You Can Rejoin Joy: Blogging for *Today's Psychology*

Volume IX in the Rejoining Joy book series

Gerald Young, Ph.D.

Glendon College

York University

ALSO BY DR. GERALD YOUNG

Research Books

Young, G. (2013). *Textbook in Psychological Injury and Law*. New York: Springer.

Young, G. (2012). *Malingering in Psychological Injury and Law*. New York: Springer..

Young, G. (2011). *Development and Causality: Neo-Piagetian Perspectives*. New York: Springer.

Young, G. (2010). *Rehabilitation Psychology [Course Kit]*. Toronto, ON: York University Bookstore.

Young, G., Kane, A. W., & Nicholson, K. (2007). *Causality in Psychological Injury: Presenting Evidence in Court*. New York: Springer.

Young, G., Kane, A. W., & Nicholson, K. (Eds.) (2006). *Psychological Knowledge in Court: PTSD, Pain, and TBI*. New York: Springer.

Young, G. (1997). *Adult Development, Therapy, and Culture: A Postmodern Synthesis*. New York: Plenum Press.

Young, G., Segalowitz, S., Corter, C., & Trehub, S. (Eds.) (1983). *Manual Specialization and the Developing Brain*. New York: Academic Press.

Trade Books

Rejoining Joy Series 2011

Rejoining Joy: Volume 1 Essays
Rejoining Joy: Volume 2 Destressing
Rejoining Joy: Volume 3 Emotions
Rejoining Joy: Volume 4 Daily Living
Rejoining Joy: Volume 5 Art
Rejoining Joy: Volume 6 The Best of Rejoining Joy
Rejoining Joy: Volume 7 Workbook
Rejoining Joy: Volume 8 Sayings

The Alpaca and Alfalfa Alphabet Book

See rejoiningjoy.com

Journals

Young, G. (Founding Editor and Editor-in-Chief) (2008–) *Psychological Injury and Law*. New York: Springer.

The 2013, 2012, 2010, 2007, and 2006 research books are books on psychological effects of traumatic events, and the like, in relation to personal injury law. The 2011 and 1997 books are on life span development. You may also consult the journal for which I am editor-in-chief, entitled, *Psychological Injury and Law*. To see my work in the area of psychological injury and law, consult the websites www.asapil.org and springer.com. To see my work in the area of self-help consult www.rejoiningjoy.com.

Rejoining Joy

Gerald Young, Ph.D.

A self-help book series
see www.rejoiningjoy.com

Text design & page layout: Beth Crane, WeMakeBooks.ca
Coverdesign: AmyGreenan, amy.greenan@gmail.com

You Can Rejoin Joy: Blogging for Today's Psychology Volume IX in the Rejoining Joy book series

Rejoining Joy Publishing Inc. Toronto, Ontario Canada www.rejoiningjoy.com

iUniverse books may be ordered through booksellers or by contacting:

iUniverse
1663 Liberty Drive
Bloomington, IN 47403
www.iuniverse.com
1-800-Authors (1-800-288-4677)

ISBN: 978-1-4759-2969-0 (sc)
ISBN: 978-1-4759-2970-6 (e)

Printed in the United States of America

iUniverse rev. date: 11/12/2012

You Can Rejoin Joy: Blogging for *Today's Psychology*

Volume IX in the Rejoining Joy book series

TABLE OF CONTENTS

ABOUT THE AUTHOR

DR. GERALD YOUNG is an Associate Professor Psychology at Glendon College, York University, Toronto, Ontario, Canada. He is also a practicing psychologist dealing with rehabilitation and with counseling. He undertakes research on two major topics. The first is on psychological injury and law [five books]. The second is on child development. His most recent book is entitled: *Development and Causality: Neo-Piagetian Perspectives* (published by Springer SBM, New York). He has written one other book, on the topic of manual and hemisphere specialization. He has received an outstanding research award from his faculty at the university. He is the editor of the leading journal in the area of psychological injury and law (*Psychological Injury and Law*, PIL, springer.com), and is the president of its housing association (ASAPIL, see www.asapil.org).

Dr. Gerald Young has gained the trust of his clients and of his professional colleagues in his professional practice in clinical psychology. He has helped numerous clients over the years; and his reports have been presented to court. As an Associate Professor at York University, he teaches students the courses of Rehabilitation Psychology, and Abnormal Child, Adolescent, Adult, and Advanced Development.

"There is unity in my university teaching, my research, my practice, and the self-help book series. With much passion, I have dedicated my professional life to the area, and the self-help books reflect that passion and the skills that I have learned and developed and want to communicate to the reader."

PREFACE & ACKNOWLEDGMENT

Rejoining Joy seems like a hard task, but these blogs from *Psychology Today* show you that it's possible and how to do it. Most of the blogs are from 2011, with some from 2012.

Sections I and II introduce the topic and help you achieve your goals. In Section III, I provide inspirational sayings. Sections IV to VI help with your relationships and how to change. Sections VII and VIII are personal perspectives meant to inspire. Section IX and X are about applications. Section XI gives last words for your new beginnings.

The people at iUniverse shepherded the book expertly through the production and promotion process. Many thanks to Jamie Mitchell, Dayne Newquist, Allison Howell, and to the Promotion & Media Department. The people at *Psychology Today* have been exceptionally supportive (Lybi Mah, and Mary Beth Lee) and deserve many kudos. The people at WeMakeBooks.ca (Heidy Lawrance and Beth Crane) put the books together for your easy reading. My office staff (Joyce Chan and Fanchea Lau) are my try-out audience (LOL). My family is always behind everything I do, too.

"Today's Psychology" is a book that is positive and hopeful for you as the reader. It is based on scientific approaches. As a practitioner, in the book I try to be sensitive to your needs.

Please visit my website, RejoiningJoy.com, to learn about my other self-help books and how they can help you.

Section I
Reclaiming Joy

HOW TO RECLAIM HAPPINESS

Rejoining Joy

Sally felt empty. Was anyone listening to her? John felt lost and depressed. Would he ever feel happy? Despite his good marks, Stan felt he had no future. Terri was worried about her relationship because her previous ones ended quickly. Jim was angry that things were not going his way. These are the stories that people tell me in my practice. Part of my therapeutic approach is to help them tell different stories, by using the concepts of rejoining joy and adopting appropriate ways of living.

All of us are deeply psychological beings. We live complex lives, but how do we live our best lives? Our daily experiences might be too difficult for us, bringing stress. Or, our past might be filled with lingering difficulties that bring us stress. Also, for any of multiple reasons, we might have bad habits that get in the way of our important goals, best values, and good habits. Further, there are biological vulnerabilities to consider, for example, those caused by injuries, accidents, illness, and others that impact physical health. Finally, we might be doing quite well, but members of our family, or other loved ones, might be experiencing difficulties that affect us.

No one is free from daily stress or from living each day as a challenge. Part of the stress and challenge that we face might be a question of perception—things might not be as difficult as we perceive. Whatever the source, many of our stresses require our best effort and coping skills. Some of us succeed, and others less so. It is impossible to stay constantly happy throughout each day. Inevitably, there are downs, or even deep feelings of being overwhelmed or having too many problems and losses. However, the stresses that we face, a crisis or danger, can be confronted successfully and our ability to deal with them can improve.

As we face these stresses, many forces could tax us or put strain on both our personal coping mechanisms and our system of supports. Stress can drag us down, can lead us to "act out," and can push us toward bad habits. It is impossible to reach a state of pure joy and stay at that level. Moreover, wanting to live continually in such a state is not a helpful goal. Rather, it is more important to strive to be on the right path to joy, even if we cannot be there continuously.

But how can this goal of being on the right path be achieved? True joy and efforts to rejoin it involve the goal of wanting to grow constantly—**wanting to grow psychologically is the ultimate joy**. In addition, stress could be a growth experience, and should not be something to avoid at all costs. When we experience distress, this does not mean that happiness automatically ends, because it could prepare for returning to it. **Life should be considered as the constant living** of rejoining joy, rather than a seeking of living in constant joy. Each time we pass through bad times and resist bad habits, we broaden and build ourselves.

The ability to rejoin joy is facilitated by having the correct attitude and knowledge. When we experience a deeper understanding of what joy is and how to get there, we can arrive at the path leading to it both easier and for longer. Having a deeper under-standing of joy and the pathway to it means having the right values, habits, and helping behaviour in place. When we live solely for ourselves and for immediate pleasures, we become continuously frustrated.

In contrast, by increasingly opening our minds and giving of ourselves, both joy and being on the right path to joy become more possible. Getting on the path to joy requires us to develop both healthy and respectful ways of living in our daily lives. Our roles, responsibilities, caring behaviour, actions, thoughts, and feelings all need to be in synchrony. Once we adopt this

attitude, stress is easier to handle and reclaiming our happiness is easier to achieve.

But how can we resist external stresses, bad habits, and wrong messages from others, from the media, and so on? We need to appreciate that we all have it in us to become the being that we want, or at least to get on the path to that person. At each moment in our lives, we have positive options that we can choose, instead of negative ones. We need to remind ourselves that there are positive choices that we can make in most any situation, that we have made positive choices before in other situations, and that we can continue making positive choices no matter what happens along our path.

In future columns, I will suggest other ways of rejoining joy and improv-ing ways of living. At times, I will refer to the scientific literature, including my own publications [www.asapil.net], or my self-help book series [rejoiningjoy.com]. Looking forward to communicating with you.

Original Published on January 20, 2011 on *Psychology Today.*
Link: http://www.psychologytoday.com/blog/rejoining-joy/201101/how-reclaim-happiness

Becoming You

Be A "BEMER"!

B	**E**	**ME**
Biology	Environment	You

You are part of the causes
of your behaviour.
The causes
are not just your genes
and your environment.

Be A BEMER. The influences on yourself are not only part environment and part genes, but also part you.

So let your "you" play its part in deciding who you are, what you feel, what you do, and how you are with other people.

Take back your life from your biology, your environment, and anything else that stops you from being true to you and being true with others.

And be a BEMER while you're doing it, in the sense of "beaming" with joy.

Tiago needed help in deciding what to do with his life because he felt so out of control of its direction. He went from job to job and friend to friend, without finding stability. He came to my office frustrated and forlorn, and began drinking to excess.

Patti felt her life was heading where others wanted it to go—her partner, her parents, and her supervisor. She came to my office depressed and stressed, and could not sleep well.

Both these patients yearned for more control in their lives. Both did not want to continue being passive about their life direction. Both revealed difficulties in their childhood related to parents who did not support them or encourage them, and who remained distant from them. My patients understood the circumstances of their parents, but it still hurt thinking back.

I explored the past issues with the Tiago and Patti, but I wanted to build a better sense of control in their lives, too, so I made the diagram accompanying this text. The point of the diagram is that instead of remaining passive and feeling that we do not have control in our lives, we can work toward creating the missing sense of control.

Perhaps for you, a sense of control is present but hidden, and just needs some change of attitude and some techniques that could be applied to keep it at the forefront. Sometimes, by examining when a bad habit or old way governs your life, and by working toward a good habit or new way, you can change for the better quicker than you might think.

However, perhaps getting a sense of control of your life is harder than you think. You might think that it should be easy to change, but it takes longer, for example, if there are serious issues in the past or if the bad habits are deeply ingrained.

Here is an exercise for you to try. Think of a bad habit that you have and that you want to replace by a good habit. Another way of saying this is to think of an "old" way that you want to change into a "new" way.

Once you have an idea of what you want to change for the better, the change has begun. All it takes is some will power to start increasing the sense of self power.

Keeping a bad habit or old way takes a lot of energy, and working through what holds you back from changing takes a lot of energy. Also, trying to explore the past could be quite painful psychologically.

However, taking the first step in the right direction leads to other steps. Have you chosen yet? Are you ready to become a BEMER?

A genuine BEMER knows that taking control of one's life is constant work. It does not end with a decision to do it, because it is a constant lifelong journey once the path is finally taken. Let me give you a few examples.

- Each new challenge presents obstacles. Sometimes they are so great that gaining a sense of control is impossible, especially at the beginning.
- Moreover, sometimes, wanting the control could work against you because it could be a great learning experience to let the situation (or other person) keep the control for the moment.

- There might be advantages for you in letting someone else have control.
- Life is a give and take of control, and wanting to live in control all the time might lead to poor decisions about cooperation, or letting others have control when the situation demands it.
- Having a sense of control does not mean that you should have control all the time.
- **Having a sense of control means that you know when it is best to take the control and when it is best to give it up.**

BEMERS, then, are BECOMERS, because they accept that

- life is a journey in which having a sense of control sometimes happens and sometimes cannot,
- they can work at increasing the capacity to know when to take the control and when to give it up, and
- they know that they are growing in other ways as that capacity develops.

However, how can you develop a greater sense of control? Once you know the plan, it is easier to put it into action. Also, in trying to change, for example, by controlling a bad habit or old way, it is always easier to add a better behaviour to what you do than trying to stop the bad habit or old way that you wish to change.

By being a BEMER, you can develop better habits and ways because that allows you to see the overall YOU better and change for the better by following the right plan. So start being a BEMER, which means start understanding that you have a voice in your life direction, your behaviours, your habits, and your ways, and also the choices that you make.

Other people can help in the task of gaining a sense of control in your life, such as in getting good social support, reading self-help books, or talking it out in a professional's office. Just ask Tiago and Patti about that.

Original Published on December 14, 2011 on *Psychology Today.*
Link: http://www.psychologytoday.com/blog/rejoining-joy/201112/be-bemer

NATURE, NURTURE, AND NOBLY LEADING THE WAY

Making Your Way In Life

The classic understanding of the origins of behaviour is that it involves biological and environmental influences, which have been called "nature" and "nurture." However, we need a more refined understanding of behavioural development—one that includes ourselves as a factor in the mix of causes that help our behaviour develop.

In the traditional view of understanding the causes of behaviour, it is neither the sole outcome of biological factors such as our genes nor the sole outcome of environmental and learning factors such as our parents, schooling, and experience. Rather, behaviour is considered the result of an interaction of genes and environment. For example, the development of intelligence depends on both the genetic influences on the brain and the environmental influences that affect learning in the child. Nature and nurture work together in behaviour. Moreover, the science of epigenetics is showing just how complex things can get—environmental factors can turn off genes, and the effects of this action can be transmitted over generations.

Although we have developed a better understanding of the determinants of behaviour in this traditional view, we need to consider that all of us contribute to the development of our behaviour beyond the influences of nature and nurture. For example, we have an innate curiosity, we have the will to understand the world, and we are active in dealing with the world. We have both a particular intelligence and specific personality, and they seek corners of the world to fit our individual needs. We have ways of coping that help us work on difficulties in our world. Therefore, behaviour reflects not only nature and nurture but also our individual selves, for example, in leading our way in the world and in acting nobly in doing so.

One truism in this area of study is that biology predisposes but the environment disposes. I would add that although biology predisposes and the environment disposes, *the individual composes.* We are the architects and bricklayers of the behavioural buildings that we construct out of nature and nurture. We are the leaders of the orchestra that composes our behaviour and our pathway in the world.

However, leaders sometimes face great difficulties. For example, each of us might somehow be disadvantaged either in our nature or in our nurture. We might have some inherited difficulties or we might have had to face an abusive world from very early in life. Nevertheless, any behaviour can be changed for the better. **We have a voice in the story that we compose about ourselves and that the world hears about us.** We can author great chapters in the narrative of the story, no matter what our starting point. All of us are like heroes who have been given difficult lots; all of us have potential for great hopes, new habits, new pathways, and new positives.

The extent to which we lead ourselves and act nobly in our effort to get on the right path and to stay on it is ours to determine. Feeling good about ourselves is not caused by external factors alone but also by an internal mindset. The internal mindset that brings hope springs from wanting to lead ourselves to better options. For example, by forever striving to keep growing no matter what the circumstance, we could grow through the worst of anything that we have to face and emerge the better for it.

Life is never fair when we think that we are owed a simpler and easier way. Life is always fair when we think that we can make it better no matter where we find ourselves and if we try as hard as we can. **Getting to where we aim to go depends not on the quality of the tools that we bring to the task but on the quality of the person that the task brings out in us.**

In psychotherapy, all patients should be viewed as having more positive possibilities and the therapist should help them become noble leaders of themselves. When my patients reach a better point in their path, I might hold up a sign from the stands that indicates, "Building your Behaviour: Nature, Nurture, and Nobly." However, they might be too busy and cheerful succeeding in their daily lives to notice.

Original Published on January 25, 2011 on *Psychology Today.*

Link: http://www.psychologytoday.com/blog/rejoining-joy/201101/nature-nurture-and-nobly-leading-the-way

Section II

Regaining Your Self

THE MAKING AND UNMAKING OF THE SELF

Calm, Peace, and Harmony Within

Jonah was in search of his identity. He was proud of his masculine side, but he wondered why he did not attract partners to share his ambition to raise a large family while he worked traveling the country. Tricia also felt confident in her self, but was embarking on a new career and had serious self-doubts about whether she would succeed. She began drinking alcohol in excess on the weekends.

Young people need to get ready for their life trip, and they are advised that it does not peak with exciting vacations on luxurious islands. Rather, life peaks in moments of calm reflection, in moving toward a serene peace within, and in following a harmonious life path.

How can you get on this calm, peaceful, and harmonious path? Even though that path might be filled with challenges that do not seem so peaceful, by striving to keep an even keel on it you might feel an increased inner peace.

Finding an inner calm partly lies in other people around you and in your environment. However, part of the answer lies in yourself—the motivation to change, the readiness to open up, the deep desire to better see within yourself and to act better with others.

The good news is that together calm, peace, and harmony are inner workings that are not that difficult to kick-start. The bad news is that they might be hard to keep once they are acquired. The best news is that we all can start building them and reinforcing them, making them key, permanent parts of ourselves.

How can you add that inner calm that we all seek into your sense of self in a constructive fashion? How can you find the ability to:

- balance your competing selves,
- bring out better your part selves that are hidden or masked and that would be beneficial to you,
- solidify those self parts that are definite improvements but just beginning to develop,
- control or even eliminate those parts of the self that really do not do you any good or harm you,
- help formulate new parts of yourself that are filled with dreams and hopes and might bring you more joy and a better way of living? and
- make sure that a critical part of yourself is the inner calm, peace, and harmony that will allow other happier and better parts of yourself to emerge and become part of you?

Sometimes you need to take a clear decision to improve yourself. You could undertake to change for the better by yourself, or get the right social support, or even get professional help. The desire to change for the better is a powerful motivation for each of us. However, **the making of your self might have to begin with the unmaking of parts of your self that are holding you**

back or are even self-sabotaging or undermining your progress.

Parts of your self that are negative might have developed very early in life, complicating the process. However, even in these circumstances, the will to change and the power that change brings might be sufficient to start you on a new path or on a path already present but modified for the better.

Can self-sabotage be so profound that any positive change is subverted? Are we destined to forever live a path that we did not choose or chart ourselves? Will we always consist of self parts that we did not construct ourselves?

Because we have good parts, hidden parts, parts waiting to be developed, and the will to grow, all of us have the potential to undo negative parts of the self, even if they reflect our own doing. Moreover, although the timing for this change might not be right, having hope that one day we can be in a position for positive change should be enough to keep us on an even keel.

By having even the start of hope and being even slightly open to positive change, we might partially break negative vicious circles in our lives at a level sufficient to create new opportunities, positive cycles in our behaviour and relations, and positive growth in self-development. Even in the most difficult circumstances, we are not destined to stay as we are, to deteriorate, or to resist any change.

We are the only species that develops throughout all the phases of our life, including throughout adulthood. Change, growth, and the potential for self-improvement over the full lifespan make us human and unique. **For each of us, changing for the better is part of our potential.** Moreover, each of us has the potential of helping people dear to us change for the better.

However, starting genuine positive change requires work as well as hope, the right environment, and good timing. You might need much reflection on the self and how you behave, as well as on the life path that you are following.

But what does reflection on the self really mean? Does it mean that we should study or work harder to get ahead, or learn how to get many friends? The dictum to which we all aim is to: "Do unto others as you would have them do unto you" (or its equivalent). What if we changed that to reflect being a better person? Perhaps we should strive to: **"Be unto others as you would have them be unto you."** Getting into the shoes of others and acting for their benefit is a great step. Being there fully for people who need us and helping with their troubles makes us better people. Sometimes improving the self means improving the lot of others, even beyond our loved ones.

Genuine giving is one way of receiving and growing. It helps you unmake the more selfish parts of the self and makes it easier to find inner calm, peace, and harmony.

Original Published on June 2, 2011 on *Psychology Today*.

Link: http://www.psychologytoday.com/blog/rejoining-joy/201106/the-making-and-unmaking-the-self

THE MULTIPLE PARTS OF THE SELF

Leading Yourself to the Stage of Growth

Dan felt he did not know himself. "Who am I? What is important to me? I cannot figure that out." He asked questions like these, and moved from one opinion about his core self to another, to the exasperation of his parents. Salem felt the same way, but she related her angst to her feminine identity and culture. "I'm trying to strike out on a different path, but family tell me what to do. They are too old country for me."

Many young people are trying to establish their roles, responsibilities, and sense of self. However, they need to accept that in all these areas changes are inevitable. Self-identity is never set as a tablet in stone, but keeps growing in one way or another. Moreover, the self consists of many parts, although this might not be apparent to us. We are used to thinking of the self as a single whole that defines us. For example, we might say that we have this particular characteristic or that specific passion.

Our sense of personhood is continually in transformation and seeking new areas of growth or parts. Even when our self seems to be stable, psychological energy is being expended to keep it in its present state. A stable self needs to ward off negative interferences or new ideas and aspirations that could affect it. **It could be easier psychologically to entertain change than to reject it outright.**

Indeed, often we strike out in new directions that might be the most chal-lenging of tasks. Moreover, after they are completed we might start out on another. That is, even though we might think that we especially seek stability, often, after getting to a stable plateau, we seek new tasks or we encounter new problems that shake our stability and move us to growth. In these cases, the self can branch out and find new areas of growth and different parts.

Of course, it might be quite difficult to confront even the smallest of tasks in the day if we are depressed, too worried, angry at life, or fearful to the point of panic and being frozen in our actions. We might have suffered greatly and cannot take the step of feeling the suffering of others. Our core self might seem overwhelmingly negative to us, with little hope on the horizon. In these cases, the self has little room to grow.

Or, we might withdraw from a task or problem, feeling that we cannot handle it, or lack resources to help us with it. We might come to believe that we cannot cope or cannot do well. We might develop a psychology of failure, or a fear of change as part of our self-concept. In these cases, the self might even become more negative, constrict, or lose parts.

When our sense of self is limited by ideas of the self that corner us in spaces with little room for positive change, how can we take back the self from these limitations, even when we have created them ourselves? Part of the answer to this daunting question is to understand that the self is not one thing but a complex of multiple definitions and parts and to seek to have them grow and diversify into new areas.

How does this concept of multiple part selves apply to you? Even though you might think that your self is a unity, and is stable and cannot change, your self might be chafing for change and growth. Your self is psychologically complex, and it could be reaching out in new directions without you being aware of it. Or, you might take a very open decision to seek out new directions in self-growth and explore new avenues in the self.

Each of your parts has developed out of your past experiences, strengths, and vulnerabilities. Some of the parts of your self might be more prominent, for example, in the way that you present yourself to other people or in how you define yourself in moments of self-reflection.

Other parts of your self might be hidden or masked and rarely become evident. One example is that you might behave in one way most of the time when you are with other people but you might behave differently when you are with a best friend.

Parts of your self that are masked or hidden are still in your core self. You need to see them as waiting for you to give them more space or time in your core self, and to have them grow so that they are more evident to you and to others.

Think of the self as having potential parts in waiting for you to activate and have grow. Parts of your self might consist of dreams or wishes that guide you at times, but are only just glimmers in the making. Or, they might be only hopes, but they still could be very powerful motivations in your psychology. These types of part selves are the ones you should try to grow, because they can lead the way for the others, and might help you eliminate or control the parts that are problematic to you. Growth can be actively undertaken; you do not have to wait for others to start changing your sense of self.

Also, there might be quite negative parts of your self that should be better controlled or eliminated. However, you might not know how to do this, or you might even sabotage all efforts to do this. Some negative parts of the self or negative habits do not go away by wishful thinking. They require much psychological work. For example, you might present as extremely virtuous and moral to others, but drink to excess occasionally, and then be rude or act even worse.

This illustrates that your self parts might be in competition or conflict amongst themselves. They might have not learned to share the stage and find balance. **No matter what happens, you remain the leader of the growth of your self, and can find new ways, paths, and joys.** Dim the lights of the stage so that you can start the next scene in the growth of your self and its parts.

Original Published on March 17, 2011 on *Psychology Today.*

Link: http://www.psychologytoday.com/blog/rejoining-joy/201103/the-multiple-parts-the-self

KEEPING CONTROL IN CHAOS

Harnessing Your Sense of Being Able

Chloe lashed out whenever she had any stress and even when she did not. Her father was like that, and she thought that she could never change. Moreover, it did give her space and respect, she thought, or was it that people were drawing back from her and were afraid to socialize with her? Her mind was a constant maelstrom of wild thoughts that came from nowhere and went everywhere. She did stay focused at work, and sometimes in her personal life. She reached a point where she yearned for something better, a serious relationship, and stability. But would her personality style let her because she had her father's genes, she wondered?

Peter seethed on the inside and would explode for the slightest thing after keeping control cool most of the time. He perceived everything as stressful or as aggressive, even when there was no reason to see things that way. He had a hard life, growing up in a dysfunctional family. He witnessed parental alcohol abuse and fighting. He and his sister would hide so that they would not get hit, too. As he got older, there were teenage gangs around, and he learned that the way to avoid them was to study in the school library. Now he worried if he could complete his education, because his anger was increasing. He would daydream acting violent, and wanted to change. But were his experiences in the past too powerful a weight to overcome, he wondered?

You are not like either of these representative cases, but you have elements that make them seem real enough to you. All of us want to learn how to keep personal control of our behaviour, emotions, and thoughts, especially when the situation demands it. However, the task of keeping self-control is difficult when there might be serious genetic or environmental vulnerabilities or difficulties that weaken your resolve. In addition, you might not have developed enough assertiveness or a core self that has learned when and how to speak up without anger and still succeed in dealing with frustrations.

The beauty of human psychology is that we are all capable of learning because we are flexible. The hard part for us is that learning is never easy, and we have to apply ourselves, especially in the hardest courses of all, those teaching concerning self-control.

Life is a chaotic stream of stimuli, experiences, and self-generated ideas and feelings. You react to not only what is in the outside environment but also to what your mind is thinking and feeling. Even in the worst circumstances, how do you keep your psychology focused on reaching your positive goals?

Each of has an able side that is filled with motivations, strengths, and solutions. **Your able side might have been put aside for the longest of time, but it is time to have it deal with your problems.** Bringing out your able side is within your ability. Moreover, seeing yourself as quite able is within your potential.

Ability is half self and half other. To bring out the able side of yourself, you could work on it and also get others to help build it. People who care for you could help, even if it is simply by listening. Others do not have to find your solutions, but solutions that come out of conversations usually reflect the input of all parties. Communication starts with one idea and usually finishes with a better one.

When family or friends are not available, you can turn to magazines, books, and other media sources for self-help. If necessary, professionals can help.

Ability can grow as far as you let it, and this includes the ability to meet the greatest challenges of life. You have that capacity to define yourself increasingly by your task-oriented and social skills. We all hear of stories of how an average person accomplished the greatest of achievements. Each of us has the potential to do better than we think or to head in the right direction.

To tower in your abilities, the tower has to be constructed one skill at time. Capacities grow through good planning, effort, energy, and application, as well as verifying how they are unfolding. Any types of distraction, interference, or intrusion are held in check.

Feeling that you are able partly stems from keeping control in the chaos around you and partly stems from altering the chaos around you so that it is better controlled. Chaos feeds on itself, and you can take measures to stop the vicious circles that grow in chaos.

Chaos can be harnessed and reoriented to what is best for you and those around you. You never know where an action, thought, or feeling could lead. Even the smallest one might lead to a chain with the greatest of consequences.

Often, bringing out ability means taking the first step. New paths open up before you as you walk those first steps out of chaos. Fogs are reminders to find free breaths. They are clear days waiting to happen.

Some chaos is good for you; it keeps you alert and leads you to improve your abilities. Too much chaos might be too difficult for you, but you need to know that it is unavoidable. For example, the worst calamities happen to most everyone at least once in their lives.

You need to prepare for the worst chaos because it will happen. However, this does not mean that you will regress because of chaos. Chaos breeds opportunity and progress as much as leading to feelings of being overwhelmed and helpless.

Being able is one side of you that can keep growing. You have the capacity to grow in many ways. For example, you work on your recreational skills, study skills, and work skills. You can also work on your sense of feeling able in undertaking these skills. Give yourself a pat on the back when you see that you are more than the chaos around you and that you can keep harnessing your sense of feeling able.

Original Published on November 16, 2011 on *Psychology Today.*
Link: http://www.psychologytoday.com/blog/rejoining-joy/201111/keeping-control-in-chaos

EMPOWERING THE PSYCHOLOGICAL CORE

Building Strength

Jordan could not believe what he had heard. His work supervisor had told him that you can feel confident in most any situation, even if it is new and anxious for you. You can even prepare for new and anxious situations so that when they come up, you feel in control.

Frima could not believe it either. She had her doubts about herself from day one. She did well in university, but no one prepared her for the real world. The courses taught her facts and theories, and perhaps how to think, but not what to do out there off campus.

Jordan was having trouble in his love life, too. The honeymoon phase was over, and his partner wanted commitment, but he felt so unsure of himself and his future. He told her that he was not ready.

Frima felt more confident about her relationship, but knew that her partner was having doubts. He had told her that—the economy is terrible, jobs are not certain, he was far from home, he felt isolated from the support of family, and he was not ready to propose. She vowed to build his confidence in himself and commitment to her, but did not know how, beyond expressing her love for him.

Jordan and Frima needed practical advice on how to believe in themselves. They might be newcomers to the world of work and to romantic relations, but this does not mean that they do not have basic skills to do very well in both. They forget that they have some base in all the lessons that life has given them up to now, including from family, friends, teachers, and their own learning experiences.

Even when life lessons are negative, they can contribute to positive psychological growth. **It is not so much a matter of what life gave you but of what you take from it and how you make the best of it. The best leapers might start out as the gangliest of kids.**

You might have had experiences that you think have scarred you, but life begins anew each day, and when you decide that it is time to begin to let go the problems and bad habits that you might have developed in your past, the present will become easier and more positive.

By knowing your core strengths and core values, you can help keep a good outlook no matter what situation you are in. By realizing that at your core there are many positives and that stress or difficult situations cannot change them for the worse, you will neither get overwhelmed easily nor feel out of control.

Getting a sense of control is not about controlling everything. Rather, it is an attitude that builds on knowledge that you can live, learn, and grow in any situation. You might have less skills compared to someone else, and surely that is true for all of us, but that does not mean that you have less potential, cannot learn to help yourself and others, and cannot improve to become your best.

Confidence in yourself is not determined only by what happens to you out there but also it is determined by what is inside you, how you approach situations, and what you think of yourself. Empowering the core starts with believing in it and wanting to have it grow.

You exercise physically, but also you should exercise psychologically. One relevant exercise for empowering the core is to imagine that you have a lack of self confidence and then saying to yourself that you will increase it by a good attitude and by learning the right skills. The first step in improving the self is *wanting* to improve the self, and the second is following through by taking the right steps. There are no magic solutions in self-improvement but there are magic beginnings and the time for you could be now.

Once your psychological core begins to become more positive, confident, and sure of itself, it will continue to grow because you will find that there is nothing more exciting or pleasurable. Gaining increased self-confidence and building better social connections because of it is the best reward that comes from working hard at self-improvement.

You will see some of the change both at work and in your relations.

But can a new positive attitude and self-confidence last? Persisting at wanting to grow is the best positive habit that you could have. By keeping on this path, you will help others around you grow in this way, too. You will learn that psychological strength means more than being firm and sure of the self because it also means being flexible and sensitive to the other (but without sacrificing the self).

Being fair to yourself and to others is the fairest way to be. Self-confidence grows when the other, such as your work colleagues and life partner, are involved in a fair way in your life. Empowering your psychological core in this way will help empower the psychological core of the people around you. In turn, the increasing strength in their core will feed your increasing core power.

Jordan and Frima are learning these lessons well. They are embarking on new voyages in self-confidence and growth. Perhaps you will meet them in your psychological and life travels as you grow in the self-confidence in your core, too.

Original Published on February 9, 2012 on *Psychology Today.*
Link: http://www.psychologytoday.com/blog/rejoining-joy/201202/empowering-the-psychological-core

PAST, PRESENCE, FUTURE

Your Time is Now

What did Doctor Young mean? "Past, Presence, Future?" I think he said that it means that I should live more in the present and worry less about the future. Also, I should not have so many regrets about the past. My friend is worse than me, because she is worrying all the time. We are both frozen about the future and have to learn to see the future as a possibility to work toward, and to try to define the best future for us.

Nothing is guaranteed, in following a questionable path toward the future, the paths most probably were not our own to begin with. Sometimes paths chosen by others for us are wickedly harmful. With Dr. Young, we explored why I have let others do this for me—choose what is best for me and where I should be going in my life. Ok, a lot of it related to my parents, and some to my teachers, with some more to my friends. But they are also struggling with their future and with choosing the ideal path that leads to personal fulfillment. Somehow, I have to see the big picture. Dr. Young told me to try to see all the influences on me. It will not be easy, but both my friend and myself are committed to change. I guess that is half the battle, to want work on the self and to work with the other.

You need to balance being inward and watching others on their path, while being outward and on a path of your choosing, but one followed with sensitivity for self and for other people as you move forward on it.

You need to find the middle ground, or better yet, a different ground, where you see at once together the past, the present, and the future. To do this, you have to learn from the past, no matter how hard it has been for you, and you have to behave with presence in the present, or with sensitivity toward the self and other, no matter how difficult that will be.

It is easy to say that your parents, or other people or events, caused this or that about you, but that is only part of the truth. **You have a say in who influences you as a person and when you can influence yourself**. Your voice can be ring truer than the voice of any other person or party about how you should be, how you should see the past, and how you should create your future.

It helps when you tell yourself that your past hurts but feeling the hurt is the start of helping yourself. Also, sometimes sharing the hurt with someone in the present helps it transform to hope, and speaking of dreams with someone might help them become more realistic and doable. Finally, it helps when you think clearly about problems in the present, see the options that might work as solutions, and choose from among the options the best one.

Future is about planning and acting on our plans, and planning is about seeing our choices and even creating better ones. By dealing with the past, the future becomes easier to see, and by living in the present, it will have a better future.

People get caught up in the moment instead of living the moment in the sense of being a fully knowing and feeling self who is open to possibility and sharing. Too often, we ask only what is in it for us instead of asking also what can we put in it from ourselves. By living a life of give and take, you will end up receiving fulfillment more than you could have imagined. In behaving this way, the future becomes easier because the present is more fulfilling.

Aside from sharing with others and thinking correctly about the self and others, self help begins with techniques that help. For example, learn how to calm the body and mind with behavioural breathing techniques. There is no mystery to it, and some explanations of it even in psychology are too complex. I explain it simply enough so that even children can start using it right away. Isn't it possible that you can learn to concentrate on the breathing passage from the nostril to the bottom of the lungs so that you are distracted from your stress and succeed in calming down? When stress returns to center stage, return to concentrate on the breathing. Add in visualizations of a pleasant scene of nature and pleasant music, if you can, to enhance the relaxation experience. By doing this, you can begin to better live the present with presence, see the past with openness, and move toward a better future. **From behaviour to thinking to sharing with others, you have the ability to help yourself and to chart in the best possible way your understanding of the past, life in the present, and pathways toward the future.**

Original Published on November 24, 2011 on *Psychology Today*.
Link: http://www.psychologytoday.com/blog/rejoining-joy/201111/past-presence-future

Section III
Sayings

THE GIFT OF GIVING

Sayings about Rejoining Joy

In the following, I give you the gift of sayings that I have made. They reflect the cognitive-behavioural and positive psychology approaches, in that they suggest that you can change for the better, but in realistic ways. For more of my sayings, check my website, rejoiningjoy.com.

You are never more than your potential, but your potential is always more than you.

Your potential might have limits but your determination might not.

The weather chills. The mind wills.

Your dreams are just an imagination away.

Horizons are her rise ons.

When you get that sinking feeling, look up not down.

Giving within your means is living beyond them.

Giving is not a loss but a joy. Giving after a loss is regaining joy.

The smile you give another extends from year to year.

Treasure hunt—Seek nothing without and everything within.

Finding yourself is seeking the other.

Everybody can use a little help a lot.

A lot of commands, demands, and reprimands get a lot flames, blames, and names.

To get good will, be good and show will.

Goodness is greatness.

Smiling unlocks worlds—laughter creates them.

Play the blame game—blame yourself and no one else for delaying your growth.

The best students graduate to studenthood.

Get that living feeling; give during the season of giving—and after.

Life is a state of learning.

Know your station in life—the library.

You don't know what you don't know but you surely should want to find out.

Knowledge and not less.

Opening to the world of knowledge can help create it.

Each of us is a fount of wisdom waiting to develop.

If you accept the inevitable, it will happen.

Paths are meant to follow—until you stop following the path.

Show me a person with an ounce of desire and I will show you a person with a ton of potential.

Standing still is losing ground.

To guarantee you won't fail, don't start.

Life comes without warrantees—so work hard for your health.

There are no lazy genes, just lazy habits.

Be the bedrock of your family—rock the cradle and give the baby peace.

In one way, strong means—not using strong means.

Harbouring hopes is a swimmingly good habit.

Loving is sharing, and sharing can lead to loving.

Bodies can come together but live apart.

The best sex is more than sex.

Lovers stay lovers when love stays love.

Living love lifelong requires living love lifelong.

To be fit to be king, treat her as a queen.

If I knew what was involved, I would have done it anyway.

Peace is not a given but a long, hard, never-ending process that takes all of you.

As the sun sets, the dusk announces the dawn as well as the night.

Just as everyone is born but not everyone lives, everyone dies but not everyone passes away.

If you touch a soul, you are never sole.

Original Published on March 15, 2012 on *Psychology Today*.
Link: http://www.psychologytoday.com/blog/rejoining-joy/201203/the-gift-giving

BAD TIMES ARE THE START OF NEW BEGINNINGS

Sayings for Growth

Here are more sayings for your consideration and living. They reflect the cognitive-behavioural and positive psychology approaches. You can change for the better using ways that fit your personality and context. For more of my sayings, check my website, rejoiningjoy.com.

Good effort and good will are the best practices.

It's not so much where you arrive but who applauds you in how you did it.

If we live to hear only the sound of applause, our mind will become tone-deaf.

Singing to yourself is an internal booster club.

Some people contemplate the universe. They should start with the drink in their hand.

The long side of taking short-cuts is that you might end up on the wrong side.

Every bit of effort adds up to multiple dividends.

When we short-change effort, we get paid back.

If I counted each and every time I sat on that couch and did nothing, the total of what is in it for me would be nothing.

Trying hard is easier than not trying.

Hard times need hardening of hard effort.

Good times are prep times for hard times.

Resting on your laurels leaves you sitting behind.

Moving up in the world starts with sitting down with the books.

Living for yourself ends up with living by yourself.

There is a fine line between success and excess—you.

Animals know more than you think. Animals think more than you know.

Nature has the answers—if we'd only ask the questions.

We are privileged guests of the planet—until we lose the privilege of being invited.

Each of us should think of ourselves as the person who might have to explain about ourselves one day to visitors from another planet.

Instead of giving your partner a piece of your mind, share it.

Love is the best ointment for hurt.

Being mean is demeaning.

Finding meaning is easier when you seek it with someone else.

Your mind is a testing ground of ideas. People are a testing ground of your mind.

We're a match made in heaven because we both try to match heaven.

The surest investment in your securities is learning from people protest power.

When everyone has a chance to reach their highest potential and help other people to do the same, there is little left to chance.

If you look beyond the next task, you might not see too far.

Distractions are good for you when they do not become central actions.

Keeping your goals in mind helps create better goals.

Goal keeping blocks wayward shots.

Mental entrepreneurs create thoughtful start-ups.

Communication is a question of knowing how to ask the other something that creates interest.

Earning genuine respect is not about how much you earn.

Taking half measures gives away half the store.

Narcisstic democracy—Life, liberty, and the pursuit of emptiness.

Pluralistic democracy—Participation makes the nation.

A society better served is a society that serves better.

Children deserve love and support to flourish. Will we flourish without giving them their opportunities?

We make the bed of polluted grass we lie on.

When we try to keep it all, there is no safety net for free fall.

Go nuclear—empower your psychological core with positive opportunities.

Just at the edge of how you think, behave, and feel is cutting-edge growth.

Original Published on March 22, 2012 on *Psychology Today*.
Link: http://www.psychologytoday.com/blog/rejoining-joy/201203/bad-times-are-the-start-new-beginnings

NATURE SAYINGS I

Inspiring Sayings About Nature

Nature is to humans as humans are to nature.

Human nature means being human with nature.

Birds sing—nature's plight.

The human merry-go-round: Round and round she goes and where she stops everyone knows.

Nurture nature naturally.

Helping nature is in your nature.

Go organic's way; or go away organics. You decide.

Keep wildlife a happy memory not a sad loss.

You can lead a horse to water but you can't make it drink, if it's polluted.

Look your child in the eyes and tell her you did everything you could to save nature.

We are part of nature—until it decides to kick us out.

We are mining nature for its resources —like in "It's All Mine."

Every good tern deserves another—But no matter where we turn there are none.

Save the planet of the apes—and the orangutans and the baboons and the chimpanzees and the...

Daddy, what's the water cycle? A long, long time ago, when there was water on the planet Earth...

And on the eighth day, humans created chaos.

Carpe Diem—while the day is still there to seize.

Every species we extinguish bides its time for our turn.

Let's hope human's survival instinct wins out over its extincting one.

Animal advice—cage your demons.

What are half animal, half human? Angels.

Do unto other animals as you would have them do unto you.

Am I my animals' keeper? Yes.

The animal bible says—humans were created from an animal's rib.

The human tornado beats the natural one.

Educate a child—Take him for a nature walk.

Name all your children Noah.

Nature's ode—Help!

Nature is man's best friend.

Original Published on March 1, 2012 on *Psychology Today.*
Link: http://www.psychologytoday.com/blog/rejoining-joy/201203/nature-sayings-i

NATURE SAYINGS II

Nature Inspires Sayings

Humans have a way with words and wars.

Animal Daily News headline—Animals convene to sanction humans.

Isaac Animalov's new book about humans —*War and Pieces.*

Animal's don't understand us. Greed Sloth Wanton destruction.

Science and art are opposite ways—of saving the world.

We are not alone in the universe—The animals are watching.

How Do I Love Thee? Let me Count the Ways
1. Don't pollute
2. Rejoice in nature
3. Save a species
4. Diversify the bio
5. Harmonize, don't harm

In the jungle, the mighty jungle, a lion cries tonight.

The Seven Wonders of the World
1. How did we make it this far
2. I'm wondering if we'll survive much longer
3. If only we didn't do that to nature
…

Food for thought—if there's any left.

Humans are grist for the military.

Occupy Main Street—The animals' protest movement.

Nature—We owe it to ourselves.

Be heavenly—Raise bees.

We are living on borrowed time—so lend nature a helping hand.

We would not be human without the animals.

Planting a plant plants a conscience.

Spring forward Fall back—As long as we can.

Nature's scorecard—Humans 1 Animals 0.

Nature should not lose hope until it's dying breath.

Nature's green message to us—If you fight the fight you'll dance the dance.

Aesop's last fable—Human extinction is not a fantasy.

Aesop's second last fable—"Why wouldn't they listen" said the carrier pigeon to the dingo.

Darwin's lament—Survival Reproduction Extinction.

The planet's dirge—Though they walked in the valley of death, they could not change.

Humans are paying their dues—carbon tax.

Humans are capable of great things— when they treat each other as humans.

Original Published on March 8, 2012 on *Psychology Today*.
Link: http://www.psychologytoday.com/blog/rejoining-joy/201203/nature-sayings-ii

Section IV
Rejoining Relationships

SEX IN MUTUALITY

From Attraction to Mutual Growth

Bill loved women, but the wrong way. He spoke endlessly about love, about himself, and everything that interested him, but he never asked his dates what they thought. He was totally into himself, and so stayed that way in his love life.

Felicity fell in love with the idea of falling in love, and moved from one love partner to the next. Once the honeymoon phases of her relationships were over, she could not handle the challenge of commitment.

Larry and Sandra had a good relationship, even in bed, but they began feeling bored and wondered if there was something missing. They were very different in their personalities, sense of security, and interests. It never dawned on them to develop shared activities and grow together.

Sexual intimacy is a psychological act as well as a physical one. In a couple, it involves two people relating in tenderness and abandon, with their psychologies meeting as much as their bodies. You have physical needs, but you have psychological and social needs, too, and all these needs meet in the sexual act with your partner.

You might think that I am carrying this too far—sex is sex and desire is desire. However, although the act might be especially physical, it happens between people, not automatons. Moreover, the period of excitement and decision to continue with and then achieve the act, is highly individual, psycholog-

ical, and personal. As you engage with a person and create a partnership that leads to sex, your humanness is exposed and connected as much as your body.

In my forthcoming book—entitled, *Development and Causality: Neo-Piagetian Perspectives* (Springer SBM, 2011)—I described five stages in human development: (1) physical development in the newborn, (2) emotional development in the infant, (3) cognitive development in the child, (4) conscious development in the adolescent, and (5) spiritual development in the adult. This manner of presenting the stages is a simplified version of a more complex model based on the models of Jean Piaget and Erik Erikson, in particular.

Based on this developmental model, I developed another one for the stages that couples go through. For relationships, I have proposed a five-step sequence of: (1) physical attraction, (2) emotional attachment, (3) commitment (facilitated by thinking through it), (4) individual growth (for example, in consciousness), and (5) mutual growth (for example, in spirituality). As with the developmental model, the stages for a couple offer a universal sequence, but one that takes on an individual character for each person.

The first three steps in this model of the development of a relationship are standard ones in the field, and the last two indicate that as you develop into a long term relationship, this allows personal growth in each partner. Then, the growth transforms into mutual growth in the partnership—each aspect of growth in one partner feeds the growth of the other partner in a growing cycle. You grow beyond what you can do on your own, because living with a partner can help you grow psychologically. Moreover, mutual growth in your relationship could involve higher-order values, such as spirituality and morality.

For each of the five stages of the relationship model, two extremes are possible. For example, for the first stage of attraction, you could be overly attracted and then shift to being overly critical. For your relationship to flourish, a good balance across these extremes is required at each of the five steps.

Let's imagine you are a therapist for two couples that need a push to the next level.

In the first couple, Ginny is totally amorous of Johnny after they first meet, and he seems perfect according to her. She is idolizing him, but is she headed for a crash landing? Or, is it him? Because once she turns in her opinion of him without any real reason, he could become too confused and forget about their relationship. By looking at the stages in a relationship that I have described, as her therapist, you might have her develop a more realistic appraisal of her dates right from the beginning.

In the second couple, you are one of the partners! You are trying to develop a sense of emotional security in the relationship, because the stage of attraction went well and you are seeking commitment. However, the game your partner is playing is cat and mouse—create trust and then undo the trust, or offer a sense of security but undermine it, too. You examine what you know of the stages in relationships, and discuss with your partner what seems to be happening. This opens up a discussion of the partner's past relationships with parents and prior partners. Because of this discussion, you solidify the commitment that you are seeking. You have helped your partner with some difficult issues that had not yet been discussed with anyone, and your relationship blossoms.

Sex goes through stages, too. It greatly reflects the attraction stage at the beginning, and helps to cement it. The highs are immeasurable, but can they last and do they lead to you wanting to give emotional security to your partner? If sex becomes a warm, fuzzy feeling as much as a physical climactic one, it helps foster great emotional feelings in a couple, but can it lead to the commitment that you so much want? Do you and your partner really seek commitment or have a love-hate relationship with the idea? If commitment is achieved, does it last, or does each partner become bored and jaded, seeking something else? Is there cheating going on, not just for physical satisfaction but for psychological satisfaction? Are you helping the other person grow and are you growing together?

Sex is part of the bonding that can lead to long term growth in a couple. But long term psychological growth in a couple—and the sharing and rejoicing in that growth—is the best way of preserving and growing the bonding in a couple. Moreover, **the sharing of mutual psychological growth in your couple could help promote the best** **and deepest feelings in sex in both partners.**

Original Published on February 17, 2011 on *Psychology Today.*
Link: http://www.psychologytoday.com/blog/rejoining-joy/201102/sex-in-mutuality

MAKING ST. VALENTINE'S DAY LAST

Your 10 Paths to True Partnership

St. Valentine's day is a day of renewal for couples. For singles, it's a day of motivation to find the right partner. Either way, we need to reflect on the nature of love in the larger sense of the word, as well as the specifics of how to find and keep love. Here is a list of ten Do's and Don'ts that will help you and your partner say "I do" throughout your relationship.

1. **Work at Love**. You always hear that you should balance work and love, but have you ever considered that love takes work and that you should dedicate yourself to love as much as you dedicate yourself to work? If you are in a relationship, do you give it the same importance as you do in your career?

2. **Love Is Its Own Reward, So Keep Rewarding It**. Love starts with physical attraction and emotional arousal, but moves to an atmosphere of security and commitment. Once established psychological growth ensues both in each partner and the couple as a whole. Love fosters and brings maturity, the best present of all. For a relationship to grow through these phases and stay at its peak, it needs both partners to focus on the other as much as the self. Stoking love leads to strokes of love.

3. **Tying the "Not" Ties the Knot**. Keeping a partner happy is not just about doing the right thing, giving the right present, or tying the right knot. It also involves growing the

right way, going beyond material things, trying your best, and stopping yourself from doing the wrong thing (such as the temptation to cheat).

4. **Be Faithful (From Bed to Head)**. You need to be faithful to your partner in every way, not just sexually. When you foster an atmosphere of trust in the relationship, it frees you from the wear and tear of jealousy and mistrust. Often, we naively believe, or just hope, that unity and sharing exist in our relationship. Yet, how can you achieve true unity and sharing in your relationship? You can create a trusting environment when you are faithful to your best ideals and life path. Your partner needs to do the same, though you might need to help the person to grow in the right direction. Keeping each other happy sexually is an important start, but trust grows when we keep each other happy psychologically.

5. **Communicate (From Lips, No Lies)**. The key to communication is to be honest, to be open, to trust the other person, and to trust yourself. When words come from the heart and mind, communication is more genuine, and more likely to bring out the best in each person. Words are powerful tools that build relationships. When words reflect what is going on honestly, you will reach your partner. When words mask lies, they hurt the other, and also the

self—even if the lies are not discovered. Moreover, the actions and feelings that accompany words are important bricks in relationship building. A look of longing could be worth a thousand words.

6. **Find the Right Psychological Position.** Relaxing the tension increases the attraction. By pulling out from a down or angry mood, you help pull the other toward you. Helping the other out of an angry or down mood helps you cements the relationship. Offering support is more important than offering gifts. Always wanting your way leads to being sent on your way. When you stand up each day to what a relationship demands, it helps make the nights last.

7. **Men and Women are From Different Planets, But End Up Here on Earth.** Although there are important differences between men and women, both sexes seek personal happiness, the right job, and success in love. Both seek the right path and psychological maturity. When they cannot attain these goals, there might be good reasons that lie in their background, in their present situation, or in themselves. On the average, women might be more emotionally expressive and men more task-oriented or instrumental. However, you never enter a relationship with an average, but with a real person. No matter what your gender, it is up to you to find out what makes your partner unique. When each partner values the uniqueness of the other person in the relationship, the relationship gains value.

8. **Be Good to Yourself and to Your Partner.** Love is not just about sacrificing for the other. Take care of yourself physically and psychologically. Control what you can in your environment. Most important, control bad habits that you know are destructive and get in the way of your relationship. A good time to start controlling bad habits is now, and a good time to help your partner do the same is a second from now.

9. **Develop a Common Language.** Communication is multi-faceted and you need to use all the channels in good ways. Talk verbally and non-verbally. Say upfront what you want to say. Behind anything you say, realize that there are many things attached that are not said out loud. Understand that males and females might put different things upfront. Think ahead to what the other person might think. Tell "big truths" and "little lies." Often, guys want sex first, but women want it to last. Work out the difference to the satisfaction of each of you. Well bedded is well wedded.

10. **Going on Dates Should Have No End Date.** Therapeutically, aside from dealing with their issues, couples should be encouraged to return to some of the good habits and feelings that they experienced in the beginning of the relationship.

You should go out on dates regularly. St. Valentine's day happens once per year, but in one way or another its spirit should animate your relationship every day

Original Published on February 8, 2011 on *Psychology Today*.

Link: http://www.psychologytoday.com/blog/rejoining-joy/201102/making-st-valentine-s-day-last

HOW TO RAISE YOUR CHILDREN NATURALLY

Rewarding Growth

George just couldn't. No matter how hard he tried, he could not sit still at the dinner table. The more he moved, the more his parents told him to sit still. The more they told him, the more he moved. Finally, they got so exasperated, they angrily told him to go to his room. He stayed there hours playing with his video games.

Ellen believed in punishment. That is how she was raised, and she was determined to raise her children that way. She was surprised when they did not tow the line. She wondered if she should just hit the children hard like her father did to her.

Discipline is the hardest part of parenting. Even when parenting is undertaken correctly, children still find ways to give stress to parents. Children could be a great source of happiness, but also they are a great source of distress.

The science of developmental psychology investigates ways of parenting children. We are learning that it is inappropriate to consider at fault either the parents or the children when behavioural difficulties arise in families. Rather, parents and children form a system, and interventions should be aimed at improving the system as a whole.

Effective parenting has been described as a good balance of being warm with children and giving them appropriate limits. Being firm with children works best when the firm attitude comes from parents who have a warm relationship with their children.

Children are different at different ages, as their cognitive and social skills grow with age. If parents apply techniques and procedures that do not adjust to their child's developmental level, the outcome could be opposite to what had been expected. For example, it will not help to offer to a child detailed explanations of why she will be deprived of an outing if she is too young to understand. Also, giving too simplistic explanations or not giving any explanation to teenagers could be frustrating for them.

Children accept discipline easier when they have developed in their first years a sense of security or trust in the world. When care giving is responsive, sensitive, and given at the right time, or contingent, children feel "lovable" and that the world loves them. As toddlers grow, their sense of initiative and independence needs careful guidance so that they have confidence in their self, their explorations, and their activities. This will help them accept moments when they have to control themselves, listen to the command not to do something or to continue with it, and so on.

Children need to learn the right time to start an activity and the right time to stop an activity. They need to learn to focus their attention, and to listen, read, watch, and so on. But also, they need to learn how to calm down, inhibit activity, and engage in quiet time or prepare for bed. Their schedules are not our schedules, and by managing their daily rhythms well, parents gain a measure of control.

Research has underscored the value of praise as a reinforcing device. It should come naturally to parents when children are behaving appropriately and should be used liberally to bring out in children both constructive activity and listening or having self-control. **Metaphorically, it seems that praise reaches deep into the mind and heart of children, engulfing them with joy and an élan to strive forth in the world with the same degree of vibrations received in the praise given to them.**

Learning. Rewards. Reinforcements. Punishments. Charts. Points. Time out. Learning theory has provided excellent discipline techniques that help shape the child to end points chosen by the parent. The secret is to know how to choose the rewards and reinforcements so that they are positive and have an effect, to avoid the use of punishment, especially corporal, and to have children understand the chart and points system. I like to use daily activities as rewards, rather than monetary ones. For example, children can get extra playtime when they listen, or lose some of that time when they do not listen. Try to avoid depriving children of a full activity, because that will lead to a sense of "who cares" and they will turn off to the plan developed with the parent.

Moreover, discipline and listening should not be just about rules that control bad habits in children. That is, children should be especially rewarded for developing good habits, such as cleaning their rooms, doing their homework, playing the piano, and physically exercising instead of playing video-games endlessly. It is easier to build good habits that leave less room for bad habits compared to trying to stop bad habits in a child where there are few good ones.

Part of what parents should be teaching children are social skills. Learning is not just about conditioning children toward goals chosen by parents. Children are active learners, and a lot of what they learn comes from watching the people and activities that are around them. When parents are on their best behaviour, children watch, observe, imitate, and learn best.

Your children are part of the great story that you are living. Narrative therapy helps us understand that you can author better versions of your story and how you discipline children. **You can learn to value the specialness of your children, find out what makes them tick, and give them the tools to tick better.** Usually, we think that parents are supposed to bring out the best in their children. However, we are learning that children can help bring out the best in their parents, too.

Children are born with different potentials, genes, family environments, and cultures. However, in addition, all children are born with universal programs for growth, no matter what are their individual biologies and backgrounds. Discipline involves not only getting children on track in the right activities and habits. It also concerns keeping them on track for positive life goals and values. The home is the crucible where the guidance needed to create the best outcomes for your children begins. Bravely take the baton that life has given you, and lovingly pass it on to your children.The way I under-

Original Published on October 4, 2011 on *Psychology Today*.

Link: http://www.psychologytoday.com/blog/rejoining-joy/201110/how-raise-your-children-naturally

BY TEENAGERS

Raising Parents Naturally

stand time is not the same as that of my parents. They say "Soon," but mean "Now;" and I say "Later," but mean "Never," or so it seems to them. What I really am saying to them is to "Chill," because what they are asking me to do will get done once my mind clears. Like, I got so much to think about in that mind of mine—so my room or my homework is the last thing that I think of.

Can't my parents put themselves in my place? I gotta worry about Me, like in, "Will he like me this way? What will she think if I dress like that?"

I am the way I am. It's not as if it's only my fault that I'm like that. There is no easy solution finding your way as a teenager. We are the between generation, no longer children but not yet adults. We still want to be taken care of like children. But we know that the adult world is looming with its demands and responsibilities. We are still trying to find ourselves and to define who we are, what we like best, which school subjects that we like, what job or career is best for us, who are our real friends, how to get that girl or guy as our partner, how to look good, how to improve our bodies, how to spend our free time, and how to earn some money.

Our social life is everything to us. It builds our self-esteem. It's not that we forget our parents. They should understand that we have other priorities now. Facebook and texting—that is where it's at.

If I'm really confused, though, I'll turn to my parents. Hey, I won't tell my friends that—they'll think I'm a nerd. But it's true; my parents do mean something to me, especially for values. If they knew how to dress like us and liked our music, I'd ask them about those things, too. But, hey, there are limits.

Speaking of limits, teenagers need fair limits. Why should curfew be so early when we go out? Parents are afraid that we'll try drugs, join gangs, get pregnant, and not think of our future. Yes, we are the Now generation, but we do want a good future, too. If our parents trusted us, now that we are teenagers, it would be better. If they explained their fears, instead of saying something like, "You have to be home at this hour, or else!" that would be better. If you ask the right way, give directions without imposing, tell us why, and have some confidence in us, that would be better.

Teenage brains are made to learn. Connections among neurons in the brain are called synapses, and the teen brain sprouts many of them that the brain then organizes. Parents think we are scatter-brained, but we are really just scattering our synapses so we can learn more, be creative, ask questions, find answers, and become better people. The teenage period is just a phase, and we get over it. So parents should get over some of our excesses and get on with it.

I wish my parents were my partners in my growth, instead of acting sometimes like my barriers. Teenagers should band together to teach parents how to raise us naturally. Here are some good pointers.

1. **Be there for us, but not all there.** Leave us some space, some independence, some free time, some dream moments. We are seeking our identities, and will try out many roles, both personal and vocational, but also in other areas. We might end up with different lifelines or paths than you, but they will be our paths and we will follow them better if we are allowed to choose them. But you can keep advising us (without nagging, please), too.

2. **Give us some responsibility for ourselves, but not too much.** We have friends that have to do it all. They take care of their little sisters or brothers, cook, clean, work, and have no time to study. No wonder they clue out, and go out seeking thrills. We are half way there, but want free time for ourselves to chill, too, so we can get energized for the second half to come.

3. **Help us, don't hate us.** We appreciate a helping hand, not a hitting one. Some of my friends were abused as children, and heard so much screaming, or worse. What you learned from your parents does not have to be repeated on us. Life does not have to be fixed, or faxed, being copies of patterns transmitted without change over generations. Rather, it could be flexible, or free, if you decide to leave your past in the past. When you grow through your worst, we can grow our best. Perhaps, if it is required, you can get some social support or professional help about this.

4. **Love us, don't leave us.** Like our style; we think we are with it. You guys were too straight. We know what is in. That music that you dislike is our music and makes us who we are. Find out why we like it. Maybe you don't like my friend for the wrong reasons. Maybe he listens way better than you do. We get frustrated, and we react. But do not reject us when we do; continue to be a part of our lives. Help us through the worst, no matter what. The home is where we belong all our lives, so keep it open to us.

Teenagers are there for a reason, to test you as parents. Please pass the exam. We will rejoice. Connection is every-

Original Published on October 18, 2011 on *Psychology Today*.
Link: http://www.psychologytoday.com/blog/rejoining-joy/201110/teenagers

INTRANET YOUR MIND

Social Tools for Better Living

thing, or at least its quantity, quality, and humanity. We have become the social media society, where we face-book as much if not more than face the books, and text messages as much if not more than finding messages in texts. We want to be linked in electronically as much as if not more than linking with each other socially, and we want to follow each other on tweeter as much as if not more than following our inclinations and curiosities in social contact and with people and with nature.

You are becoming so adept with social media, but what will you do when living connected electronically leaves you no more room for living connected in face-to-face contact? What will happen when the preferred form of dating is predominantly virtual and fantasy-saturated instead of vital and fulfilling?

You might decide that you are overwhelmed and return to more traditional, natural ways, such as smiling to a real person, and cultivating genuine friendships. However, instead of retreating from the electronic world, one option to follow might be to intranet your mind.

Behaviour reflects the complex interaction of biology, environment, and ourselves. The environment includes cultural influences, and the niche in which human evolution had taken place is as much cultural as anything else. Moreover, the cultural component can evolve

very rapidly, as we are witnessing with the social media under discussion.

However, despite the hype, human social contact, such as happens in dialogues and in interactions involving groups, remains the best source for learning about the social world and behaving in it.

One way of understanding and appreciating social media is to consider them adjuncts or additions to your social world rather than the core or center of your social world. The balance has to swing back to the human side from the social media side in social communication, or you risk losing necessary social skills or not even developing them. **In your communications and social life, if you ignore the human side for the expediency of the machine side, you risk losing the human side and becoming hostage to the machine side.**

The intricacy of human interaction across multiple channels, both verbal and nonverbal, including in the dynamic coordination across two or more people, is stunningly complex. The quadrillions of connections in the human brain allow this ongoing, finely-tuned human interaction to take place. Also, the environment (especially through parents and other caregivers, playmates and friends, and schools and other educational venues) helps promote and refine these connections. However, you have a major voice in how much and how well your brain and its neurons interconnect and how well your environment is responsive to you—though your choice of activities and acquaintances, motivation and studies, curiosity and readings, and so on.

Here are some strategies for improving the connections both in your mind and with other people through the workings of social media.

Intranet your mind. By this, I mean be aware that all the different parts of your psychology require interactions of a genuine social nature, and not just a virtual nature. Do not lose perspective that social media should be means for social contact and not just media contact.

Internet your mind. By this, I mean that once you take the step of becoming constantly aware of the human side of communication, you will be able to use the internet and all social media as add-ons in your social life rather than replacements.

Socialize choice. A vibrant mind keeps seeking new ways and exploring all options possible in each situation. You should decide to live by "choosing choice" so that your behaviour is always the best possible in any one situation. Moreover, choosing choice means choosing people. Your mind cannot think in isolation. Indeed, thinking is a social act requiring others in shared exchange on the best options to follow in situations, and most situations of importance are social and communicative ones.

Find your "grow zone. Grow your brain, behaviour, body, and mind. Find the "grow zone" in these regards that works for you, and keep the zones genuine. Live a healthy lifestyle by making healthy choices in all these aspects. But that is another story.

Original Published on February 24, 2012 on *Psychology Today.*
Link: http://www.psychologytoday.com/blog/rejoining-joy/201202/intranet-your-mind-0

Section V
Repairing the Self

TEN PRINCIPLES IN PSYCHOTHERAPY:
BUILDING HOPE

Being a psychotherapist is a fantastic responsibility

Imagine a mental health professional starting the first session with a new patient. The patient could describe extremely difficult problems to the therapist, or those problems as described by the patient might be just touching the surface and mask extremely difficult issues out of awareness of the patient.

Problems such as these illustrate that being a psychotherapist is a fantastic responsibility, and requires much education, training, and experience to be successful. In my practice, I have found that some basic principles make it easier for both myself and my patients.

1. The first principle of psychotherapy that I follow is that a new patient should not be viewed only from the lens of the personal problems being shared with the therapist, whether or not they hide deeper issues. Rather, each person in psychotherapy should be viewed as a whole person with a unique personality and lifestyle, and living in a particular context. Each patient has personal strengths that the therapist needs to discover and bring out in the patient, even if these strengths are masked by the problems of the patient.

2. The second principle in psychotherapy is that it works best when there is a good match between the patient and the therapist. The therapist needs to have good rapport-building skills and should speak at the level of the patient, keeping in mind that each patient is unique.

3. The common myth is that psychologists can read the mind of people. However, behaviour is too complex to grasp quickly and clearly all the reasons underlying it. As mentioned, the real problem facing the patient might be very different than the one described by the patient (for example, one partner could greatly misrepresent the problem in couple).

4. Fourth, the therapist should assess the readiness to change in each patient. Patients might resist good suggestions, sabotage their progress, not cooperate, and so on. The therapist needs to be attuned when a patient is more open to change and should guide the patient toward it. The therapist should be alert to when a patient is not ripe for change.

5. Fifth, the therapist should assume that patients deeply want change, even if there might be resistance to varying degrees. **Having hope and wanting to change for the better is the human birthright**. The therapist needs to help the patient unlock the power of positive change.

6. Sixth, the patient is the one that has to do the changing. The therapist can only be the facilitator, or provide

the scaffold. The therapist can help the patient see new habits, paths, and ways of being, or more positive stories to tell about the self and the future. However, the patient is the one who must choose these new options.

7. An important principle of psycho-therapy is that each of us, no matter what our age, can grow psycholog-ically. As human beings, each of us is in continual transition to a better path and to a better way of being. We might get stuck at a particular level, or even regress. However, the therapist should work from the principle that problems are solutions waiting to happen. Therefore, the therapist should work from the assumption that each moment in our lives is a moment for potential growth. **We should never stop believing that our problems can be solved or that our growth cannot continue.** By adopting an attitude that living is about transition and trans-formation, we can get through the most difficult times.

8. Aside from the positive grand narratives that therapists can help patients tell about themselves and the future, therapists can also teach specific techniques and procedures that can help patients. For example, in the behavioural tradition, patients can learn both relaxation exercises and the scheduling of positive events and activities. From the cognitive tradition, they can learn not to think so negatively, pessimistically, or catastrophically. Also, they can learn particular social skills, for example,

to control anger or, at the other extreme, to counteract shyness.

9. The ninth principle that I adhere to in therapy is to keep it simple. Much of therapy is putting together techniques and concepts that reflect common sense and folk psychology. Science helps determine what works best, and the therapist needs to be able to keep up with the complex literature. However, the basic principles in psychotherapy can be communicated to patients in simple terms without losing much information. For example, in my practice I indicate to patients that I follow the approach of "action and distraction." That is, I describe psycho-therapy as learning positive ways of living, or engaging in positive activities. Furthermore, when we are not being active, we should distract ourselves from our stresses, for example, by learning positive ways to relax, reclaim joy, and reduce stressful thoughts and feelings. Another principle that I describe to patients is that of "surrounding the negative with a positive." For example, after telling someone an inappropriately critical comment, one could tag on a more positive statement or a reframed one. After telling someone what to do in a too forceful way, one could add, "Perhaps that is a good idea and what do you think?"

10.Finally, there are overarching or superordinate principles that help explain behaviour and how to change it when it is problematic. For example, I view behaviour and its change as reflections of the principle of "activation/ inhibition coordination." Therapeutically, this principle refers helping patients to *activate* or initiate more positive actions, thoughts, feelings, ways of living, and stories about the self and the future. In addition, it refers to helping patients to *inhibit* or interfere with blockages that can get in the way of new habits and lifestyles. Patients need to have hope, as do therapists for them. When psychotherapists understand their patients and how psychotherapy works best from a scientific perspective, it is easier for them to instill hope and have hope.

Original Published on January 25, 2011 on *Psychology Today*.
Link: http://www.psychologytoday.com/blog/rejoining-joy/201101/ten-principles-psychotherapy-building-hope

UNIFYING THE DIVIDE WITHIN

Competition and Cooperation can Cooperate and Not be in Competition

Winning is everything. Good guys finish last. May the best team win. Champions are built on teamwork. These are some of the proverbs that reflect the universal tension between behaving as an individual to get ahead and blending into a group to get ahead. In the following, I examine the opposition between competition and cooperation as one example of the oppositions that we confront in our psychology, and how we can deal with them by working toward their integration.

Both strategies have their benefits, and we have to learn to combine them into a blended strategy of adaptation. Competition and cooperation work best when they fight least, that is, for a place in our mental space.

The roots of competition and cooperation are in our biological heritage. In one sense, Darwin conceived of evolution as involving survival and reproduction by means of winning competitions. However, scientists today are also focusing on group processes in human behaviour, such as taking the perspective of the other person, altruism, sharing, and working for the common good.

Moreover, life is not just about winning. The goal should not to be on top in everything that we try to do. Rather, it should be to ensure that the foundations of wherever we find ourselves in our work and in our personal lives remain on solid ground.

No matter what the competition, we need to respect the other competitors and other people in our lives. For work, this refers to co-workers who are in lesser positions of authority. For our personal lives, this means communicating with sensitivity to our loved ones, partners, children, parents, siblings, and so on. When we look at life as cooperation as much as competition, and try to blend the two, the balance that we reach might be more manageable and fruitful in the long term.

When winning dominates your psychology, the prizes that you obtain might be fleeting and empty. However, when your goal is to keep competition in balance, so that it does not dominate your life, you end up winning in many ways, although it might not be monetarily or in terms of other material benefits. By keeping your sense of self intact and by not stooping below standards of decency, you always win in the development of your positive side.

You can learn to balance competition and cooperation and have them work together. For example, adults can work together in brainstorming on the job, and the result is that the company makes financial gains so that work positions are more secure and there is more room for advancement. Or, you can share in day care activities and in bringing children to child care.

The younger you are, the more likely you are competitive or are engaging in cooperative behaviour for personal advantage. However, the focus on giving selflessly grows, and the child, teenager, and then adult become freer and more flexible in doing so. You become better at combining competition and cooperation For example, you become sensitive to the other person, but without sacrificing your sense of self and your interests.

People should view you as neither competitive, pushy, self-interested, and egotistical, nor as self-effacing, easy to push around, and without personality. Rather, people should view you as having a unified self in terms of this competition and cooperation. Ideally, you will become cooperative, constructive, and communicative while keeping control of a competitive "edge" that you might have without losing your assertiveness.

However, ideals do not always guide reality. If you are especially competitive and want to win at all costs, it will be difficult to be genuinely cooperative and build toward the integration of the two tendencies. Or, if you are only paying lip service to one side, there will be slip-ups and leakages that will give

you away and you will get the opposite of what you are seeking.

The sooner that you balance these oppositions, the easier it will be to move beyond them and keep on a positive path. Competition and cooperation can cooperate and not be in competition. You might have to deal with the hardships that accompany any effort to grow, but the unity that accompanies success in the task will help heal the divide within. Finding balance in these types of oppositions is critical to self-growth. Facing life means engaging in its complexities and being open to possibility.

Life gains meaning when you gain perspective. Life peaks in meaning when you can place all perspectives in a unity. Life keeps its meaning when you try to improve the quality of the unity that you create.

Therapeutically, the task of joining opposites can proceed with shared conversations with the therapist about the oppositions. For example, once on the way to unity for competition and cooperation, it would be easier to deal with finding balance in other oppositions. You could navigate difficulties with issues such as security/ insecurity, dependence/ independence, and trust/ mistrust. **Becoming a whole person involves dealing with the**

Original Published on June 23, 2011 on *Psychology Today.*
Link: http://www.psychologytoday.com/blog/rejoining-joy/201106/unifying-the-divide-within

THE SELF AND THE OTHER: FINDING BALANCE

Seeking Identity in Re-Responsibilities

divides. Jennie had it with her parents. They wanted her to stay home, not go out with her friends because they were not like young people back home. She was 21 and wanted more freedom. She wanted her parents to trust her. Junior had too much to do at home, as his parents were so busy. He longed for the time he could do just what he wanted.

Shandra felt she was part of the lost generation. She took drugs, flirted with too many boys, and felt that she was getting nowhere in her life. Ron wanted more from life. He was raised in an affluent family and socialized with people from his family's social class. If his parents gave money to charity, there was always an underlying reason related to themselves, such as getting social approval. Ron wanted more than to look good in the eyes of others. He wanted to look good in his own eyes, and to aspire to a better moral life.

Jennie can learn to balance modern ways and the old ways of back home. Junior can find time for himself and for his parents. Shandra and Ron can give better direction to their lives—Shandra by reaching for a more moral plane and Ron by acting on his moral side.

Young people are sandwiched between their past lives as adolescents in which they probably had less demanding daily responsibilities and more free time, and their future lives as adults, which might seem forboding and not just challenging. They appreciate their increasing independence and move-ment toward their own lives, but they find it difficult to find their way. It is hard for them to feel that they are living their right path. There are so many choices to make, so they might feel lost.

For example, can you find balance in your work and studies, and in your friend time and the time for your partner? You are exposed to temptations, such as drinking alcohol, easy sex, and risk-taking behaviour, but can you manage to avoid them? In your search for fun, you might forget about family and culture, and fixate totally on the self. You might have become too self-indulgent and there might be little mental space for considering the others around you. Or, you might be in a posi-tion where you have to give too much to others, such as family, and have little time for yourself.

However, in our culture you need to find balance as individuals with a personal life and as people with responsibilities, such as in the family and at work. You need to harmonize the individualistic "Me" and the collec-tive "We." Erikson described develop-ment in terms of stages that consist of oppositions or poles, such as identity establishment vs. difficulty in construc-ting identity in adolescence. A danger is that you become too focused on one side of the challenge, for example, by continually seeking your identity at the sacrifice of everything else or by stop-ping to seek your identity.

Young people join the parade to self-growth into the mature adult easier when they do not ignore the other. When self and other are in fine balance in the attitude, mind, and behaviour of the person, it is easier to feel complete and to undertake the responsibilities of life as an adult with aplomb and success. When young people balance autonomy and interdependence, or the Me and the We, they make headway.

Erikson referred to the adult stage as involving generativity. He did not mean this solely in terms of generating a family. Rather, he meant this in terms of caring responsibly for the family, working responsibly to support it, and also giving of the self to society beyond what one gives to the family, within one's limits. The French philosopher Emmanuel Lévinas also emphasized the importance of responsibility in the adult.

In my own work (in my 2011 research book; in my self-help book series), I conceptualized the sense of responsibility that one should have as an adult as "Re-responsibilities." For me, Erikson meant generativity to refer to adopting an attitude of responsibility for each major life task, and doing so continuously and well.

Therefore, your task as an adult can be defined as being responsible in everything that you do, and renewing the commitment to being responsible at each moment of your life. Being responsible demands your constant renewal because of the difficulties involved, the temptation to think it is too hard and to let it go, and the changing context of your life.

You will find life easier when you gladly live its obligations, even when they become difficult. In living life this way, you will find it easier to experience the greatest of joys. For example, as a young person starting your adult life, you will realize one day that the smile of a child to the parent can lights up the universe inside you. The thanks sent by a co-worker for helping out can make your day. Two hours spent at the community center helping the poor can enrich you forever.

Moreover, if you try to avoid responsibility, you lose so much.

- First, by trying to avoid responsibility you lose its joys, such as your child smiling to you.
- Second, genuine joy comes especially when you work for it in one way or another. The pleasure of accomplishment surpasses any pleasure obtained without trying to get it.
- Third, accepting responsibility and applying yourself to it allows you to grow psychologically, which is a great joy.
- Fourth, rededicating to all your responsibilities on a continual basis means that you have grown so much and it allows you to grow so much more.
- Fifth, the inner calm, peace, and harmony acquired by living the path of Re-responsibilities leads to a balance in your self and in your identity that surpasses any other joy.

Original Published on August 16, 2011 on *Psychology Today*.
Link: http://www.psychologytoday.com/blog/rejoining-joy/201108/the-self-and-the-other-finding-balance

POWERING PERSONAL CHANGE

Starting and Stopping on the Way to Greater Joy

Sarah wanted to change right away, and change everything at that. She sought advice from everyone, describing endlessly her problems. She tried many solutions, but her problems did not diminish. She was told to have patience and plan, but she could not even take that first step.

Stan believed that his problems were so complex that he could not change. He kept his worries to himself and did not even try to improve. He was advised to take a step-by-step approach, but he did not know where to start. Finally, he tried a small change, but was disappointed that it did not help and he stopped.

Change begins with the will and the want to undergo it as much as taking the first step toward it. It is not one point on a line but walking the full line.

Change proceeds in stops and starts, and once it reaches one level, you do not proceed right away to the next. If you wish to keep the change in the long term, you have to see how it is helping, and act to keep it. You must consolidate the change, get used to it, and have it become a stable part of your good habits.

The same principle applies each time that you make a positive change. There are many forces that could undo it, including falling back into bad habits that the change is meant to replace. **For psychological change to last, you must work at it.** As it becomes more ingrained and part of your behaviour, it will become automatic, and you

will be ready for the next step. Moving forward psychologically is as much preventing moving backward psychologically. By giving change a chance, much of your behaviour could blossom in widespread change.

You might be asking yourself: How you could contemplate positive change when you feel so utterly down, or when a negative behaviour is so built in that it has become a major part of your psychology?

Change could start with a miniscule seed that reaches majestic dimensions. Change is like the sands of the beaches of the world. Beaches are filled with grains that create beauty, but each grain is tiny and unnoticeable. You need to see the beauty that a collection of small changes can bring and put them together.

Change proceeds in steps and, although each one seems so hard to achieve, together they work to give you a more positive psychology, better habits, and an inner satisfaction. You should tell yourself that for change to begin and grow, a small step might set in motion a large change. Therefore, it is worth getting on the path to change and keeping on it.

One model of change envisions that it takes place in a series of five steps (in my book on development and causality, Springer SMB, 2011; the stages are called: coordination, hierarchization, systematization, multiplication, and integration). In the following, I present the model in terms of replacing bad habits or old ways with good habits or new ways.

1. In the first step in change, you move beyond your sense of stagnation of not experiencing any change and your sense of being overwhelmed without the capacity to do anything. You have a vision of how it could be better, and you imagine it, seeing yourself adopting good habits or new ways. You perceive the bad habit/ old way and the good/ habit new way side by side, and the contrast sets the stage for adopting the good habit or new way.

   Therefore, the first step in positive change is to take the first step! By seeking different habits and ways, by seeing how the different ones would be better than the one you want to change, by selecting a feasible option among the choices, and by sticking to the new choice, you can make that first important step in positive change.

   For example, if you want to exercise more, you start with the will, and then you go slow to begin, building up the effort over time. Similarly, if you want to develop a good habit or new way, you start with a wish, and then you should go slow in developing it and building on it.

2. In the second step of positive change, you practice the new habit or way so that it is a real part of you or of what you do, even if it is just a small part. For example, in developing an exercise routine, perhaps you do only five minutes of exercise each day. Or, in developing better anger control, perhaps you do deep breathing exercises and tell yourself to watch your irritation before you answer back to someone.

3. In the third step of behavioural change, you make sure that the good, new way is a strong part of your daily behaviour, and that you see how it can help even more. For example, you add new exercise routines. Or, you develop the right way of dealing with someone who has irritated you; the techniques that you are using give you some self-control and the time to think.

4. In the next step, the positive psychological change spreads, because you see the advantages and try out change in other areas. Perhaps you are motivated to socialize more because you feel better physically and psychologically from the exercise. Or, perhaps you exercise more, because you see the changes that you are making in your control of irritability and want to feel better physically, too.

5. In the last step of change, you realize your desire to achieve wide-spread change, at least for one major area in your life. There is no turning back, and the new habit or way is harmonized inside the core self and manifests consistently in your behaviour. You are ready for major changes in other areas now that this improvement is in place. At this point, you realize that change for the better is the best.

Original Published on November 8, 2011 on *Psychology Today*.

Link: http://www.psychologytoday.com/blog/rejoining-joy/201111/powering-personal-change

Section VI

Automaticity and Authenticity

AUTOMATICITY AND AUTHENTICITY

Gaining Flexibility and Freedom

No matter what she tried to do to change, Tricia lapsed into her bad habits. They were deeply anchored in her, having developed in her childhood when she was abused. She began drinking in her early teens and never could stop, no matter which professional she consulted or which advice she followed. She was lucky to keep her job, but worried for the day when she could not function there any more.

Victor tried to help her but he was having his own problems with drinking, especially when he combined it with marijuana. The highs used to be great, but he found himself getting increasingly paranoid and depressed as he indulged. He went to a group dedicated to abstinence, but knew he was fooling himself. However, when Tricia told him that he was part of her problem, he tried to stop but did not know how. Then, they drank together even more.

There are many other examples possible where you might have difficulty either letting go of bad habits or replacing them with better ones. Also, you might relapse into bad habits even after having let them go. Daily life is a constant struggle to stay focused, work, study, take care of children or elders, as the came may be, and remain on an even keel in the evening after the day. The day might give you immense stress or little time to relax, so the end of the day might be when the stress affects you. For example, that is when you might drink, or argue with your partner, or be nasty to the children. You know that you are capable of more but bad habits are hard to break even if you know they are unhealthy for you in the long run.

What are the reasons for your inability to put aside bad habits, especially when you want to change them? First, they might give immediate, short-term advantages. The first drink might be relaxing. Yelling at someone might relieve some stress. Also, because the roots of the bad habits might be deep and have developed from negative experiences in childhood, they might be familiar habits that are hard to put aside, if not impossible, without help. You might not even recognize them as bad habits, or refuse to believe it when others tell you that they are harmful to you or hurtful to others. Even if you put them aside, they might be lurking in the background, and you might always be wondering if you really have overcome them.

The chains that bad habits might create make your behavior appear automatic in the sense that the bad habits keep repeating no matter what. Despite your best efforts to go beyond them, they might always come back. No matter how much you try to try something else, they appear without thought, as if in a reflex action. Their hold on you is complete, and you are never free from them.

However, reacting automatically with bad habits that might have a powerful anchor in your behavior does not have to happen automatically each time. For example, you can begin to cut back drinking a bit, or remove yourself from the room in which an argument seems to be developing, by asking for a breather (not a breathalyzer!).

Taking the first steps to free yourself from automatic habits is the first step toward becoming more present in the moment, or more flexible in behaving with other people. When you are fully engaged in interacting with other people, you are communicating and behaving from an open stance that can adjust well to whatever comes up. There is nothing holding you back from being fair to yourself and to the other people who are involved. One way of describing this approach to social interaction is to call it genuine or authentic.

Think of two poles that are far apart with a long clothesline between them. Moving from the automatic pole of behavior to the free, flexible, and authentic pole would take a lot of hard work, and you might have to stop to rest and so the clothesline might slip back a bit despite your best efforts. Moreover, the line might slip not only because of the efforts needed to keep it advancing but also because it is attracted to the automatic side due to some sort of energy force, which is a way of saying that past bad habits still have a hold on you, for example, due to things that had happened in childhood such as abuse.

Imagine trying to pull a clothes line that is buffeted by a strong wind. This could represent the situation of trying to move from the automatic to the authentic pole of behavior and interaction in difficult contexts, when the day has been long, and so on. But also, imagine that a howling hurricane over the horizon is sending bursts of overpowering wind your way, too, and that this represents difficulties from the past. These second types of wind could pull you toward automatically using bad habits and could stop you from moving toward better habits.

There is no easy solution to navigate the behavioral dimension of automaticity and authenticity, especially if your life has been difficult up to the time that you decide to improve and to move toward authenticity. In my blog entries, I have emphasized that deciding to improve is half the battle and getting on the path to improvement is the other half. Being on the voyage is the voyage. The end point is a hope and a goal that helps, but the end point is a moving target so the voyage never really ends. How much the person can improve and knowing the starting point where the improvement can begin varies from person to person. **Improving is not a race but a movement.** Once the voyage toward authenticity begins, there are many ways it can continue. Many people and sources of information such, as self-help books, can help.

When you can look in the mirror and feel more relaxed about yourself because you are becoming less automatic in your behavior and more open to what is happening in the present, you will feel freer from the past and happier in the present. You will be less defensive and have less of a shell around you. You might discover aspects of yourself that you should keep improving, and some discoveries about yourself might hurt. However, people will notice your movement toward authenticity and social bonds will be created that will help both you and them. The increases in your authenticity will help move others away from their automaticity, in a mutually beneficial and positive process. Perhaps the moment to begin this great movement in freeing yourself from the automatic toward the authentic is now. Tricia and Victor probably agree.

Original Published on April 5, 2012 on *Psychology Today*.
Link: http://www.psychologytoday.com/blog/rejoining-joy/201204/automaticity-and-authenticity

LIGHTING AND LIGHTENING

Moving Toward Authenticity

Trianna felt a lifeless burden on the inside pulling her down. It felt like a dark region in the middle of her self that stopped her from being herself. She was sure people noticed and that they wondered what was wrong with her. She wanted to change and become happier, but did not know where to begin. Her husband and child would be happier too, she thought, if she could only start.

Billy was wild and knew it. He enjoyed his reputation as someone who could not sit still and who could not be counted on. He felt that there was a pounding, heavy drum keeping away the calm side. But after his last brawl in which he had his lovely nose broken because he had tried to bum a cigarette, he decided that he should shape up and get a job. However, he asked himself where to begin.

Probably, you recognize these scenarios or know people who fit them. You might be a person who is more internalizing and prone to depression and anxiety or you might be a person who is more externalizing and liable to get angry and in trouble. However, each of us has both sides to different degrees even if one predominates, so it is best that you learn how to deal with both of them when they get out of hand.

The best strategy you should use when your behavior is at the extreme is to seek the middle ground. If you are too internalizing, you should concentrate on what helps to make you brighter on the inside instead of darker. If you become too externalizing, you

should do what it takes to act with more restraint and feel lighter on people instead heavier on them.

Lighting and lightening are strategies that can lead to more balance in both internal feelings and outer actions. The doom and gloom can become more zoom and boom, and without being overbearing and aggressive with people. Or, the anger and troubles that follow you might recede so that you become more regulated and motivated.

You might jump from one side of the equation to the other, and go from being externalizing to internalizing, or vice versa. If your mood pendulum swings quickly like that, it might be hard for it to find more balance that lasts with little effort. It might be exhausting for you to fight the extremes in your mood and behavior if you do not know where you can find the middle and how to get there.

Many of your attitudes, actions, thoughts, and feelings are automatic ones that repeat because they are easier to use and they have worked in getting you through the day. However, as much as you keep repeating them, they never seem to work all the time in helping you in the situations of the day. Indeed, sometimes they cause either you or other people great distress. Think of your supervisor or boss coming down too hard on you and you just take it and try to learn what he wants. However, when you get home you break down and cry and no one can help. Or, think of your colleague trying to take advantage of you and you automatically tell him off, even though the supervisor or boss is nearby. Later in the day, to try to relax, you need a few drinks, but you clue out when your child asks for help with homework.

The behaviors and ideas that you have might be automatic because you want to chunk or reduce them after they become habits that you use frequently, so you can use them without thinking too much. This process is adaptive, or good for your psychology, because it leaves you room to learn other behaviors and ideas.

However, other types of automatic behaviors and ideas develop because they stop growth rather than help it. For example, in becoming less automatic, you might free buried memories that seep through with the lifting of the automaticity in behavior. Freeing one part of behavior to gain flexibility might free other parts that you might have wanted to stay buried because you are not ready to deal with them, the time is not right, they are hurtful, and so on. Indeed, they might have been buried so deeply in your psychology that they are unconscious memories and normally you are not aware of them and they are not accessible.

For example, you might internalize not only because it is part of your basic personality tendencies but also because you had been abused and had to be quiet during the abuse to the best that you could, or it was so depressing each time it happened. In contrast, you might externalize because it is more than a basic personality pattern of yours—for example, you had been hit so hard so many times as a youngster

that you developed a rage that now comes out easily.

In either case, you could have continued to get on with your day as a child, go to school, not share what was happening with your teachers or classmates, and so on. As the teen years passed into the adult years, your habitual ways of dealing with people and problems became automatic in either the internalizing or externalizing direction, or both, You buried the causes as too hurtful to confront and the people who caused your suffering as too difficult to confront.

When you begin to realize that the time for positive change has arrived or that you should prepare for it, there will be a world of hurts that might be released and some that are totally unanticipated. You might uncover deep secrets about yourself or your family, aside from learning about the hurts that you had felt and how vulnerable seemed your life and the world. However, **in the process of wanting to change, you will learn how much there is a positive side of you that wants to grow and come to terms with the past no matter how hard it is going to be. You are your best change agent.** Other people and sources can help you, but the great voyage of change is yours to undertake. Once it starts, you will sail into the brighter seas and lighter waves of your future.

Trianna and Billy have started out on their trips of change, and the seas are leading to a middle ground in their mood, attitude, actions, and thoughts. This ground is a surer one to stand on, and people will feel comfortable standing on it with them.

Original Published on April 12, 2012 on *Psychology Today*.
Link: http://www.psychologytoday.com/blog/rejoining-joy/201204/lighting-and-lightening

FROM AUTOMATICITY TO AUTHENTICITY

Dealing with the Hidden and the Forbidden

Automaticity in behavior protects you from (a) past problems that are too difficult to face, (b) stresses in the present that are overwhelming, and (c) the need for too many changes in our usual behaviors because of changing contexts or times. Automaticity in behavior does not refer to putting aside your psychological and social life as you complete tasks that are important for your day, such as at work, in school, or with your children. Rather, this refers either to distancing yourself from emotions, hurts, and paths in the past that have left indelible marks on you or to overwhelming stresses or demands for change in the present that are too difficult to confront.

However, in the short run, in all these cases the loss of flexibility in behavior could hinder your ongoing adjustment. Moreover, in the long run, they could do serious harm to how you confront problems and stresses, which could have important implications for your psychology and your personal life. When you are out of touch with your internal feelings, hurts, and frustrated hopes and goals, they fester like internal psychological sores and can do further damage.

There are many ways that you protect yourself from extreme psychological problems, whether they come from your past or your present. You might use psychological defenses such as putting a psychological barrier around yourself so that you do not feel the hurt or the stress. This might be a useful strategy in certain ways, but there are costs to you, as well, such as not getting fully involved in the situation or trying to resolve it.

In fact, things might slip further out of control despite your best efforts to gain control. For example, if you have lived a lifetime this way because of abuse or the like in the past, the emotional distancing might be quite strong. However, your blocked emotions could also leak out unexpectedly in situations and, moreover, what leaks out might not be very adaptive and could be too negative.

Therefore, you might deal with problems by trying to ignore them or to not deal with them directly, and this could lead to long-term patterns of letting things go. In the end, this type of reaction leads to the problems and stresses dominating you and to having you adopt a passive strategy when they appear.

Or, your typical reaction might be not to let things go but to overreact and let nothing go. If you act too strongly against problems and stresses, when that type of reaction is not called for or only makes things worse, you are really being passive rather than active, in the sense of the problems controlling you and how you react to them.

If you go the opposite way and wear your emotions on your sleeve, so to speak, your emotional reactions might be too strong, misplaced in the context, or even the opposite of what you should be doing. If you might lash out and get too involved, your behavior will be nonproductive and discourage finding solutions.

The examples provided might be describing you very well, and one way of summarizing them is that they reflect automatic reactions to problems and stresses rather than more flexible responses. The more you are automatic in how you deal with problems and stresses, the less you are able to respond well to them and the less you are able to foresee them and to head them off with good strategies and plans.

In contrast to behaving with automaticity, you could behave the opposite way, or with authenticity. I have called having a full and free flexibility in behavior authenticity because when you act without automatic chains to past behaviors that do not fit the present problem or stress, you increase the chances of finding the best solutions.

When you avoid habitual reactions that are inflexible and automatic in situations and behave instead in the opposite way—with responsive actions that seek solutions to the problem or stress in a controlled way—you increase the chances of adjusting better to the situation. Also, other people will be more likely to perceive you as more free and genuine instead of chained to past habits and inconsiderate of them.

By acting with authenticity rather than automaticity, positive cycles in behavior and social interactions could develop rather than negative vicious circles.

However, changing behavior so that it has less automaticity and more authenticity might be a long, hard struggle. For example, when you move a psychological rock holding you back, what if you find buried under it hidden traumas or forbidden secrets that hurt? As a child, you might have experienced major abuse and you had to put aside its harmful effects in order to get on as best you could at school and at home.

By starting the change process in moving toward authenticity from automaticity, you will have taken the first steps in regaining an active approach to living rather than a passive, reactive one. The benefits in taking steps to move away from automatic reactions to active authentic actions greatly outweigh the costs involved. Moreover, in confronting the past hurts and harms, help is at hand in people around you, resources that you consult, professionals who might be available, and readings that you can begin.

When the hidden and forbidden become open to exploration and help, gradually you will feel a greater inner peace and a calmer way of dealing with people. Dealing with secrets frees the chains of automaticity and the freedom of authenticity.

Original Published on April 20, 2012 on *Psychology Today*.
Link: http://www.psychologytoday.com/blog/rejoining-joy/201204/automaticity-authenticity

Section VII
Injury and Illness

PSYCHOLOGICAL INJURY

Is There Real Trauma, Pain, or Brain Damage?

Karen felt so depressed and traumatized. "Oh my, I do not know where to turn. I can't smile anymore. My co-workers are wondering. My daughter worries and tries to cheer me up. I cry for no reason. I wasn't this way before the accident. Why did that kid run in front of my car? I keep dreaming about it, how they tried to save him. I keep having nightmares it is my daughter." Karen exhibits all the major symptoms of Posttraumatic Stress Disorder (PTSD), including the feeling that she is reliving the accident (flashbacks), nightmares, jumpiness, reacting to reminders, fear of driving, hypervigilance when driving, poor sleep, and relationship numbness. Her family doctor sends her to a psychologist.

Jimmy could not stand the pain. "I used to be on all the school teams. Rugby was my favorite. I was team captain. I was looking forward to playing on the university team. Now I am in a wheelchair with a crushed leg, and my dreams are crushed. Why did the driver drink and drive? He gets away with a ticket. I lose my life." Jimmy has developed chronic pain and depression because of his accident and the serious changes in his quality of life and activities of daily living. He is not motivated in his rehabilitation. A psychologist is called in.

Frank had part of his skull sheared off and received a facial smash as well as multiple injuries. His friend took him on a joy ride on a country road, and lost control. They hit a tree. His friend died. Frank was in a coma for 2 months, and ended up with serious brain, sensory, and bodily injuries. His mother never accepted the doctors' prognosis that if he survived he would be in a vegetative state in a group home. She remained by his side day and night for years, coaxing him on. He is now completing his high school diploma through the home study program that she organized with the school board, although he needs 24 hour care. She indicated that she would not have succeeded without the help of the psychologist who the case manager had contacted.

Paul found me by looking in the telephone directory. He claimed that he had a serious car accident, and hurt his back and leg. He limped and used a cane. I listened to his complaints but was doubtful because of his extremely exaggerated pain behaviour and inconsistencies in his story. He failed a psychological screening test of whether he was "faking" it. I declined to see him further. I had read that week in the newspaper about criminal elements starting up rehabilitation clinics and staging fake accidents.

These stories are based on true cases that I see in my practice. They have been changed in detail to protect the privacy of the individuals involved.

People who are hurt in accidents suffer physical and psychological injuries, and after comprehensive assessments I might diagnose PTSD, Major Depression, chronic Pain Disorder, or refer to a neuropsychologist to evaluate for possible Traumatic Brain Injury. It is harder when the patients suffer polytrauma, or two or more of these conditions together. They might also manifest an Adjustment Disorder, which is less serious, or other anxiety disorders, such as a Phobia of driving vehicles.

The cases are complex when there are pre-existing factors, such as a personality disorder that has not been treated, a pre-existing psychopathology such as Bipolar Disorder, or ongoing stressors that predate the accident at issue (e.g., a divorce that has been conflictual). In addition, psychologists might have to deal with patients who grossly exaggeration their symptoms or even are lying or malingering for financial gain.

Fortunately, psychologists can use tests that help in determining not only clinical problems but also when malingering or related behaviour might be taking place. These tests include the MMPI-2 and the MMPI 2 RF (Minnesota Multiphasic Personality Inventory, second edition, Restructured Form; chief author, Dr. Yossi Ben-Porath). However, the tests are not fool proof.

Moreover, psychologists might have to give testimony in these cases, and the need to remain impartial is required. (Note: when psychologists evaluate these patients for court purposes, without preparing reports for treatment purposes, they are called forensic psychologists.) However, the pressures of the legal system might influence their approach to the testi-mony (these pressures are called "the adversarial divide").

Generally, psychologists are empathic to patients in rehabilitation and treat them effectively. Moreover, forensic psychologists, in particular, evaluate them comprehensively and impartially. However, both types of psychologists face difficulties when a patient is dishonest or when they face pressures from insurers and attorneys.

The best remedy for psychologists and other mental health professionals in dealing with these stresses is:
* to be educated and trained to an excellent level,
* to practice the profession with integrity (as per their professional regulations and guidelines, such as the Specialty Guidelines for Forensic Psychology (Committee on the Revision of the Specialty Guidelines for Forensic Psychology, 2010; chief author, Dr. Randy Otto), and
* to be up to date on the scientific literature on which their practice is based (e.g., the journal *Psychological Injury and Law*). Their professional and governing bodies and their patients expect nothing less.

Today, I was asked if it is depressing to hear these stories from patients. To the contrary, it is uplifting when I hear how they are improving with therapy and can take the small steps (and sometimes great leaps) in their recovery that I try to help them bring out. The task of treating them might appear overwhelming, but **psychology is a scientific profession that has developed finely-tuned treatment approaches and specific procedures that can be** tailored effectively to meet individual needs.

The best way of helping patients with these injuries is to give them scientifically-informed treatment, but only after verifying as best as one can that their psychological injuries are genuine and not grossly exaggerated or the result of lying or malingering. Fortunately, a majority of patients are honest. They might be crying out for help, and psychologists are well-trained to offer the help that they need.

Original Published on August 29, 2011 on *Psychology Today.*
Link: http://www.psychologytoday.com/blog/rejoining-joy/201108/psychological-injury

POCKETS OF JOY, CAVERNS OF PURPOSE, MOUNTAINS OF HOPE

Rehabilitating Polytrauma

Shauna's and Dave's accident was so serious that the police had wondered how they could be alive. A tractor-trailer truck had been too close behind them when they had to stop suddenly to avoid an accident that was taking place in front of them on the highway. The huge vehicle rammed into them, going over the back seat of the car. Their twins were 2 years old then, and in their child's seats buckled up. Shauna was rendered unconscious for a while, and she suffered disabling back injuries. Dave fared better, getting just whiplash, but he froze in fear seeing his wife leaning on his shoulder unconscious and in not hearing the children in the back once the truck stopped. He looked in the rearview mirror and saw the truck. He was too afraid to check if the children were alive. Then, to his relief, they started crying. He still had decapitation nightmares. His wife did recover consciousness before the ambulance arrived, and was diagnosed later with a concussion, or mild Traumatic Brain Injury. However, she never recovered enough to return to her work in accounting, especially given her pains, headaches, sleep difficulties, depression, anxiety, PTSD, chronic pain, and cognitive difficulties. The couple's intimacy was greatly affected. The family doctor referred the couple to a psychologist.

Robin was 8 when the accident happened, Darlin 3, Billy 6, and Belinda 6. The parents died in the accident, and family helped raise them. The children suffered serious injuries and burns, and were treated for this for years. The intense heat in the accident is one more factor beyond all the physical impacts that seems to have affected their brain functioning. I worked with them throughout their childhood and teenage years, and they were quite traumatized and numbed. They tried to forget about what happened, but locked it in or denied that it still affected them. They became quite inward but, as they got into the teenage years, they acted out. They required a full rehabilitation team for all the years of the treatment. They remained quite depressed and struggled with school and career choices, although all the help that they received had given them a future as adults. However, they needed counseling throughout their early adult years, and beyond. Each new crisis in their lives required more intense psychotherapy.

Andrea lost her child in her accident. She was not hurt much, but her son was evicted from the vehicle, as the chair snapped from the impact. She suffered terrible nightmares and flashbacks, feeling as if she was reliving the accident. She set up a "shrine" about her son in his room, and withdrew from the world. She felt so guilty even though the accident was not her fault. All her past psychological difficulties re-appeared as serious problems, as well, and had contributed to the development of a prior personality disorder that had never been treated. I tried to instill some hope and have her stay focused on her remaining children. However, her long-term prognosis was poor. I could not use the standard cognitive behavioural techniques, offer her hope, and help her accept and move forward. She needed a high dose of anti-depressants. She never could return to the work force. Her other children suffered from her withdrawals, as she was a single mom. Social workers had to be called in.

When there are complex psychological injuries that touch the body, mind, and brain, psychologists use complex treatment procedures that address them all. Moreover, we examine in detail the daily life of the individual and how it has been impacted by the accident in order to help in adaptation. What are the changes in the functional activities of the person, such as in work, and homecare? How have leisure activities been affected, as well as family life? We explore quality of life, activities of daily living, sense of well being, and so on.

Also, accidents are not the only way people might need the services of psychologists for physical and psychological symptoms. Patients might be suffering from illnesses. These might have psychological consequences, such as depression, or they might worsen when depression is present.

The body and mind work together in disease. Psychologists refer to the biopsychosocial model. That is, the physical conditions of patients are influenced both by their psychology and by their social environment. For example, the more that they have good coping skills and good family support, the better should be the outcome.

Whether dealing with psychological injury due to accidents or psychological conditions that accompany illness, psychologists adopt standard psychological approaches, such as cognitive behavioural therapy and interpersonal therapy. The former helps find the triggers to maladaptive thoughts, so that they can be changed and lead to improved behaviour and mood. The latter works on social skills and relationships in context. Rehabilitation psychology is special in the way we work in teams, as required, such as with physicians, occupational therapists, and physical therapists.

There are other valid psychological approaches in rehabilitation, such as narrative therapy. What are the negative stories that patients are telling about themselves and their future, and how can they be changed? Can patients write or author new chapters about their lives that are more positive in outlook? For example, how can a tragedy be a growth experience, even in a minor way, if not more?

One way of summarizing the approach that could help patients in rehabilitation is to have then realize they can change their psychological GPS to a better direction and they have the ability to do so, given what has been learned about their strengths and the positives in their progress to date. One way that I might inspire patients is to refer to helping them find pockets of joy, or even caverns of purpose and mountains of hope. Using hopeful language can help inspire hope. The approaches of positive psychology and finding solutions are very helpful with patients in rehabilitation, and they illustrate the progress being made in the field.

Original Published on September 3, 2011 on *Psychology Today.*

Link: http://www.psychologytoday.com/blog/rejoining-joy/201109/pockets-joy-caverns-purpose-mountains-hope

"IT'S CANCER!" I WAS TOLD.

Could I Rejoin Joy?

The words that I have cancer still resonate when the hematologist told me. The first response that I had was to ask, "How long do I have?" He answered that most likely I won't need chemotherapy for a few years because it is a slow growth one. After the shock, I continued with my life as best I could. I continued to work at the university and at clinical office as a psychologist and I continued to publish, which is my pride and joy. However, in my moments of fatigue, the worry would set in like a cancer itself.

Moreover, it took only 8 months for the hemoglobin level to reach just above the level that indicates the need for chemotherapy. It fell 12 points in 2 months to 102, and I only had a 2 point-margin for the next time. My children were in their 20s and 30s, and I had grandchildren, I thought, and my wife was a university professor, as well, so I worried less about them and more about completing my life tasks.

In particular, I had a child and life-span development book that I had wanted to write from scratch for the professional audience and a psychology self-help book series to complete for the public, as well as making sure that the society and academic journal that I had just founded were launched effectively. I was two hemoglobin points away from strong chemotherapy, and I had no guarantee that "chemo fog" would allow me to think clearly enough to finish my life tasks.

I decided to complete my projects no matter what. My condition is non-Hodgkin's lymphoma and it was too early to tell which kind. There are 29 different kinds of NH lymphoma, and some are worse than others. I was told that when my hemoglobin level would lose 2 more points and reach 100, I would get a bone marrow biopsy. It would help determine the exact type of NH lymphoma that I had and then the right chemotherapy course could be plotted. I learned that 18% of people pass away from NH lymphoma in the first year, and my levels were going down quickly, but nothing would stop me, I thought. I was used to working daily at the university and the clinical office for months on end, and I said to myself to just keep going. I also knew that one's attitude was crucial in keeping on course in cases of serious diseases and injuries, and I determined to be positive. It proved harder to stay positive in moments of fatigue, but I persisted.

Not only did I owe it myself and to my life projects to keep going despite the diagnosis of cancer, as well as to those who would be helped by their completion, but also I owed it to my patients. I had always told them that they had a choice to be more positive and to work through their stresses, despite their pains, injuries, or illnesses. In addition, I taught them cognitive and behavioural techniques, we practiced them, and they used them in their daily lives. I emphasized to them that you always have at least some control of your life no matter what your circumstances, and it came natural for me to adopt the same approach. Moreover, this was the basic theme of my self-help book series and even of this blog for *Psychology Today*—**you have a choice to rejoin joy and to reclaim happiness even after the worst stresses and tragedies.** Moreover, **you are active agents in your psychological growth—you are not just reflections of your biology and your environment but also reflections of what you decide for yourself.**

Cancer became a word for me that meant, "I can, sir!" I am not suggesting that you have the same work drive as me, but any drive will help in circumstances like mine. Passions of any sort can help deflect worry and depression, feeling helpless and hopeless, and wanting to stop. Good activities keep the mind relaxed and focused and stop it from dwelling on negatives. Be a warrior against stress instead of a worrier and its ally. Also, psychological techniques and therapy can be powerful adjuncts in your quests to improve yourself and the life of others. Psychology informs the best ways of living. That principle animated has all my writings and clinical practice, and it came to characterize my own dealings with my diagnosis.

The world might be three-dimensional, with time considered the fourth dimension. However, your universe contains a fifth dimension, and it consists of how far you look beyond the horizon both at work, or in other daily roles, and at home, and how hard

you work in realistic ways toward getting there.

Well, I just completed my projects; the book is written and the self-help book series completed. The society and journal are on firmer grounds, as well [www.asapil.net; we are still seeking members and donations to this non-profit, :)]. I use material from the book in my child development university course and material from the journal in my rehabilitation course; also, I use these ideas in my clinical practice. So the way things have developed form a nice unity, I thought. I had held off the disease long enough despite the precipitous drop in my hemoglobin level in its first year. Perhaps it was not mind over matter, but surely the attitude of my mind was part of the solution.

Disunity began when my hemoglobin finally fell below 100 a few months ago, just after I had finished the book; I was called in for the biopsy. A few weeks ago I got the results—the news was terrible. I was told that I had Waldenstrom's—a rare, uncurable cancer that is nasty. Unity crept back in the picture a few days ago when a second opinion indicated it could be a milder form of NH lymphoma. My hematologist respects the opinion of the first doctor, and I am on a month-to-month watch now, in case. My hemoglobin moved back to the 100 level in the last check, and of course, I hope that it stays there forever.

As I entered this year, the one for which the doctor had predicted I would need chemotherapy, I have become more reflective and I have been expressing my thoughts in these blogs. For example, I thought of what I should tell students, in particular, and therefore wrote my blog entries on why I love science and why we are all students of the world. My next blood test is in a few days, and I wondered what I can tell you, in perhaps this last blog, depending on the test results [although I have about 10 other blog entries in the hopper, including another reflective one on "WikiWaysofLiving."]

In moments like these, of course, spiritual matters become important. I found solace in the support of family members, in particular, and that was enough for me. Despite the ups and downs of life, my path has been a pleasant one to date, I thought, and I was thankful.

I hope this story contributes to your spirituality and having a positive, hopeful attitude. We all have a sense of spirituality and of goodness that binds us to ourselves and to each other. If you are in need of exploring further how to develop a positive outlook, you might want to consult my blog entries and my other writings, such as self-help book series. Rejoining joy is your birthright. Its journey never ends.

Original Published on September 27, 2011 on *Psychology Today*.
Link: http://www.psychologytoday.com/blog/rejoining-joy/201109/it-s-cancer-i-was-told

Section VIII

Personal Perspectives

SPIRITUALITIES

Connecting with the Universe

Having a sense of spirituality is different from being religious, although often the two overlap. Having a sense of spirituality belongs to everyone. It is not a property of external sources such as religions that bestow it on us or need to teach it to us. Rather, it is a property of ourselves that we can nurture by our connection with entities or to an entity greater than ourselves, such as a believing in God or feeling oneness with the universe. We might feel spiritual in connecting closely with the people around us, with nature, with our sense of a supreme being or beings, or with whatever we attune to in this way. In addition, our sense of spirituality could grow by connecting with more traditional religious thought and sources.

In brief, **our sense of spirituality is about feeling connected**. People might have a sense of spirituality without being religious. Or, they might be religious without having a sense of spirituality.

Being given a diagnosis such as cancer gives shock but also it gives hope and determination. It raises spiritual issues, too. Typically, we pray for ourselves and for our loved ones but also for our nation or even the whole planet. For many of us, in praying, often we are asking the supreme being for the use of special powers to help us or even to save us. It could be that there is a healing God, and our prayers will be answered. However, what if in a religious sense our relationship to a supreme being cannot lead to special favors for us, despite our wishes?

Moreover, we could imagine a religious belief system in which our relationship to a supreme being or beings is not for the purpose of gaining advantage for ourselves but is exactly the opposite! That is, it could be that a good way of thinking spiritually is that it is up to us to help or even save the supreme being by being good, noble, moral, and helpful. Of course, God could be a healer, but this would not deny that we should be healers, too, and that we might even be His best healer! In the remainder of the essay, I examine this latter possibility and its implications.

Religiously, we might think of our relationship with God in terms of an all-powerful figure who can respond to our prayers. However, it could be that we are the only ones responsible for our behaviour and for our predicaments and also that we are the only ones responsible for finding the needed solutions or those who can help us. In this sense, if we are too dependent on trying to seek help in a passive way from all-powerful beings instead of seeking help from ourselves in an active way, we might miss opportunities in how we can help ourselves and in how we can get others to help us.

The argument is simple: Perhaps the all-powerful being to whom we pray does not respond to our prayers. Instead, we are the ones who are responsible for ourselves and for others, and even if He intervenes it might be to make sure we know that. Moreover, the argument might go one step further. Perhaps our responsibility even includes taking care of or growing the supreme being or beings to whom we worship or pray, including when the belief system involves God! That is, it is not that God needs to take care of us and be responsive to our prayers. Rather, **perhaps it is up to us to take care of God and be responsive to His prayers. And what might His prayers be? Well, I would guess that He asks each of us to take care of ourselves and of each other, as well as of our environment, including the whole planet, so that His work reaches its maximum potential.**

By thinking in this new way, whether from a religious or spiritual perspective, we might realize that as we improve in our actions, in our thoughts, and in our feelings, we become more godlike. Also, from a religious perspective, it is possible that as we improve this way, God improves because He is limited by the degree of our improvement. That is, when we are best, He is best, but when we are not, He cannot.

Therefore, from a religious point of view, it could be that God's development reflects our development. When our behaviour, thoughts, or feelings decline in quality, so does His level of development. He suffers when we do not grow.

The conclusion of this train of logic is that, from a religious point of view, God's suffering is in our hands; it is not the other way around. When we hurt someone, it is felt deeply by God. He bears the scars of our misdeeds. It is up to us to nurture Him back to health. When we stand upright in the difficult world around us, God raises His hands to the heavens and thanks us.

From a religious point of view, we learn to pray for special favors and for help from God. However, it could be that as we mature we need to act god-like instead of asking for God's intervention in our affairs. Erich Fromm wrote: You shall be as gods. However, from a religious point of view, it could be that when we act at the highest levels of goodness, not only are we acting as gods, also we are growing God in ways parallel to us.

The same message applies from the spiritual point of view. **Goodness brings a sense of "godness," and our goodness is unending in its growth potential.** Therefore, our collective sense of goodness and "godness" can grow without limits. We need to make the world around us a better place at all levels each moment that life has given us breath, or at least have that goal—from family to neighborhoods to society and the planet.

The universe is ours and ours alone to improve. Doing so in each moment of our lives—by the goals that we adopt, the actions that we take (admitting that we cannot work at them endlessly), and the feelings that we share—makes the universe a better place for ourselves, for each other, for our children, and for their future. I refer to this as accepting and undertaking our re-responsibilities, by which I mean that we need to recommit and dedicate ourselves to our multiple responsibilities in each moment of our lives. By doing so, God or whomever or whatever we pray to or attune to, can get the help needed and, therefore, we shall be as gods.

Psychologically, the message of this blog entry is a useful one. We are responsible for ourselves, for our behaviours, for our habits, for our thoughts, for our feelings, and for our attitudes. We can be our best agents of change when things are not going well for us. Spirituality is one way of seeing a better way. We should foster it for its helping potential. Moreover, if possible, we should try to avoid types of thinking and traditions that mask it and weaken its power.

Original Published on March 29, 2012 on *Psychology Today.*
Link: http://www.psychologytoday.com/blog/rejoining-joy/201203/spiritualities

STUDENTS OF THE WORLD

We Are All Students Of The World

We are all students of the world. First, we are all students no matter what our age. We live in a learning laboratory that is life. We are exposed to the best teachers—experience and each other. We could be the best learners, should we keep the curiosity and motivation that animated our childhood, which might have been either in front of books or before the glories of watching ants in the grass.

Students in college and university are doubly blessed. They are at the peak of the learning experience from the cultural perspective and they have the energy and yearnings of youth to propel them into the world once their education stops. However, it never realty stops. Their idealism needs to be fostered at centers of education as much as anything else. Society should nurture it rather than worry about and canalizing it. We should raise our children not to be in our image but to have their own and to impress their stamp on the future so that it can continue.

Second, we are all students who are exposed both to the wonders and hurts in the world. The majesty of nature from which we all issue has bred in us an equal majesty in our intellect and knowledge quest, our passions and compassions, and our desire for improvements in what we see and how we act. Part of that mission is to give back to nature what it has given us. Sometimes, we are too taken by our daily lives to have time for anything

else. However, our beings breathe in all aspects of life around us, and even if nascent or dormant, we all have the capacity to learn the magnificence of nature, suffer in how it is harmed, even by us, and strive to remedy the harms. No one can do it alone, but we cannot act together without the collective of each of our voices vibrating in unison.

The universe sings primal rhythms that our science and technology is beginning to decipher and it provides the chorus to our life. We need to place ourselves in the middle of those harmonies, and contribute to its music. Sometimes we have to withdraw into ourselves and reflect and other times we have to spread outward from ourselves and have others reflect on us. The back and forth sways of our meditations and activations constitute the flow of life. It is cemented by a mindful and peaceful interior presence that radiates into our daily contacts and touching. We need to learn to control influences that detract from this mindset without damping the energy and exuberance that accompanies it.

Students are graduating this time of year from many levels of institutions of learning, from elementary to post-graduate. Your parents and guardians are justly proud. However, you face an uncertain future and elements beyond your control. Although you are striving to be at the center of your world, you begin at the margins. How can you assure yourself that you have some say in reaching your goals?

First, you need to define your goals and, as this essay is arguing, they should include wide visions beyond the daily struggles of finding the right job and surviving the day. **Living in balance makes walking the tight rope easier and even helps find good ways to get off it.**

Second, you need to live your life, not your goals. The balance of daily living means that you are not dizzied by trying to reach the end but are aware of the present and what it needs for it to go as best it can. The ends do not justify the means; this truism has to be balanced by another that the ends help define the means so that they need to be upright, with vision, and part of a wider life field in which you and others share a common and noble future.

Third, keeping a positive outlook helps in any situation. In addition, preparing for any situation helps keep a positive outlook. Practice makes perfect, they say, but I say that practice is perfect, and whether it ends perfect might be beyond our control. Moreover, change and modify what you practice to fit the changing times and circumstances. Evolution avoids convolution.

In their convocation addresses, students want to be assured that life will unfold with their dreams intact and that their motivations are sufficient for the tasks at hand, given all that they have put into their studies. Granted, you have learned academic and technical skills, but these must be nurtured continuously in lifelong learning. Moreover, although you have not received marks for the people skills that

you have acquired in the last few years, they constitute an equally important acquisition in the course of your formal education. Modern technology is linking you in social networks, but people skills are face-to-face skills. Family and friends, colleagues and co-workers, and so on, are your best teachers. Listen, validate, learn, and grow. Other people can help us do that, and we can help them.

Communication is not just about two people in dyadic exchange. It is also about groups of people communicating (countries, communities). Students can help different communities communicate through their vitality, creativity, and skills. By continually learning at this level, students can help the fundamental rhythms that flow in the universe smooth out its discordant notes. **Let the learning symphony of the world begin anew each day for each of us, because we are all students of the world.**

How can this essay help you as a student, you may ask. It is you who has the answer. In each question lies the elements of answers that you or others acting together can find. Each question is an entry to a universe of questions, so never stop asking. Each question can bring forth answers that have never been proposed, and that can help you and others who have helped to find them, so never keep seeking. In other words, **always remain students of the world no matter what your age, and both you and the world will keep growing for the better.**

Students learn critical thinking skills that cut across classes and disciplines. However, critical thinking does not only mean being critical in thinking. It especially means being careful in your thinking, considering all the factors involved in a situation, and what might be the best solutions. Critical thinking is also about creative thinking, thinking boldly, and thinking morally. Our generation had bequeathed you life and we want you to think critically for us where we have not. That is the best way that you can be students of the world for us.

Original Published on July 11, 2011 on *Psychology Today.*

Link: http://www.psychologytoday.com/blog/rejoining-joy/201107/students-the-world

INTERNAL WORLD WARS

From Abuse to Community

In the following, some of the language is shocking, but it is meant to help each of you improve some of your worst negative thoughts about other people, from children to romantic partner, to groups such as minorities. In improving this way, you will be improving yourself psychologically. I describe five ways of thinking about other people, and you should be moving toward the upper levels as best you can.

1. In internal WWI, abuse was perpetrated with ease. Children were violated. Partners were raped. Enemies were eviscerated. And the perpetrators felt no remorse. Rather, they felt unburdened and powerful. In their eyes, there were no real victims, because only other humans can be victims, and the violence unleashed against the others in these cases was perfectly justified and not worthy of losing even a moment of reflection or doubt. Those who suffered at their hands were considered of no importance, and were called the worst derogatory names possible. In their eyes, pests and vermin should be treated better. The survivors of their acts had but one option, to accept in silence.

2. In internal WWII, the aggressors dominated the victims. The latter were not abuse or killed without hesitation, but their lives were made very difficult and unacceptable. Children were viewed as objects of suppression or subjugation. Partners who might have wished for some expression of freedom were repressed. Peoples under their sway were opposed and lived under an authoritarian regime. Life was full of impositions and manipulations at the receiving end and the major thing expected was that the sterilized or filtered knowledge that they received was accepted without question.

3. In internal WWIII, people were partially treated without abuse or domination. However, they were channeled and pacified, so that any hint of resistance was bought out. The rewards available to them were aimed at their bodies, not their minds, from money to availability of the basics for survival. They were tantalized or seduced by these offerings, and became docile or quiescent in their lack of freedom. Children followed the rules, and did not make waves, having learned that severe punishments awaited them, or rewards were greatly reduced. Partners suffered in silence, and accepted with glee the pittances given them. Minorities in countries were exposed to discriminatory and assimilatory pressures, and had a hard time to manage.

4. In internal WWIV, great progress was made, but the other was still partially considered a threat who should not be given full freedom and democratic

rights. Those in charge worried that their own limitations would be exposed. Parents worried that their children would criticize them for their remaining limitations. Partners expressed a desire for growth with and through the other, but found that their stated goals were subtly undermined or even had them sabotaged outright. Minorities in countries were given much toward living in full freedom and the chance to participate in democracy, but there were subtle pressures limiting them.

5. Most likely, you are growing toward this fourth internal psychological state in the series of five being described, or you are in it already, and hope to reach the next one. In internal WWV, children, partners, and people are all treated as part of a larger community, worth preserving and growing. For example, in the family, members work to empower each other, to bring out the best in the other, and to grow as best as one can. Equality and emancipation are passwords for everyone in these communities, and ideals become reality.

What are the consequences in behaving each of these five ways for other people around you?

1. No one will submit forever to despotism and obliteration, as in internal World War I. This type of attitude will create a chaotic response in the hope of evading and even destroying the source of the oppression.

2. When people live a regime of subjugation and authoritarianism, as in internal WWII, their pent up frustrations can lead to revolution. They seethe in anger, and develop a cognitive filter that could lead to unprovoked explosions.

3. Resistance is the nom de guerre of those who live pacified, crude lives under an assimilatory regime, or at least resistance could develop once the emptiness of their lives become evident. Instead of doing everything that they are told, they could find underhanded ways to resist, and yearn to escape the life that they have had created for them, despite the temptations included in it.

4. **People who appreciate a truly free way of living, but still encounter some impediments, will try to advance, but if the barriers are too high, they might turn inward or get confused, only to try again.** They do not want their consciousness limited, or their genuine freedoms constrained. They have noble goals, and they try to integrate them into their life at all levels.

5. In the last step in the growth of the internal world, the task is to keep on top of the gains at each moment. A second goal is to assist others to do the same. One danger is from the inside, as the will and ability to keep at the highest levels wanes. Another danger is that there are societal blockages stopping people from living according to this philosophy.

Each of you has these five internal world wars inhabiting your minds, relations, and future. You have it in you to move to the highest levels through the five steps, no matter what you have experienced in the past and no matter what society that you live in. Other people can be your partners in moving toward this internal and external peace, including family, good friends, and even therapists.

Based on the concept of "the cognitive (mis)perception of the other." See my book: Young, G. (2011). *Development and Causality*. NY: Springer SBM.

Original Published on February 16, 2012 on *Psychology Today*.
Link: http://www.psychologytoday.com/blog/rejoining-joy/201202/internal-world-wars

Section IX

Positive Society Psychology

POSITIVE SOCIETY PSYCHOLOGY I

Improving Our Well-being

You are living in most troubling times. At the economical level, worldwide economic crises threaten your way of life and governments across the globe are incapable of quick fixes. At the political level, different regions are marked by discord and by wars large and small. At the climate and geographical levels, catastrophes surge and the struggles of daily survival is a constant theme for many. In your neighborhood, the elderly fall sick, people lose their jobs, marriages cannot hold, children suffer in silence or they act out, and the school system might be overwhelmed. However, there are not enough medical and social services to help them out.

Psychology offers approaches and therapies that might be beneficial for helping society as a whole. The stresses that are all around us affect your sense of well-being and might worsen psychological tensions, vulnerabilities, and disorders that you might be experiencing. You are not immune from societal and global pressures and tragedies, and cannot insulate from them. They add to your daily dealings with work, family, social institutions, and other people. However, when you are in distress and need to consult psychological supports, such as self-help books or even counselors, the science of psychology has developed a range of effective ways of helping. Moreover, they might help you deal with outside pressures for which you have little control. Further, I am proposing that approaches and techniques that help individuals and their families can be useful in helping society as a whole to improve.

Psychotherapy

In a 2008 article, I reviewed the major approaches to individual psychotherapy, and emphasized that we should be treating the whole person in context. The problems that you might have are not just on the "inside" but also reflect your relations in the world, from work to family to society. In individual psychotherapy, psychologists use the cognitive behavioural and interpersonal approaches, in particular, and increasingly are using approaches such as positive psychology and narrative psychology. The classic approaches of psychodynamic and learning theories also have their role to play. As well, I had argued that the biopsychosocial approach is a good one to keep in mind.

In addition, psychotherapists need to be aware of the person's developmental level, family or partner, gender, culture, and groups with which he or she might identify. At its most basic level, individual psychotherapy attempts to replace bad habits, thoughts, and attitudes with good ones, to increase one's sense of well-being and relations with others, and to assure that means are in place to keep the gains made. My own contributions to understanding psychotherapy have been to call it transition therapy and activation/coordination therapy, partly because you are always in transition no matter what your age and therapy is about activating good habits and stopping bad ones.

Further, an essential component of successful individual psychotherapy is that the therapist establishes rapport with the patient and a supportive environment to facilitate positive change. This allows the therapist to deal with the darkest problems and moods of patients and even confront them about their failed solutions to their problems in an effort to establish new ways of being, relating, thinking, and feeling.

Society

The same principles that I have described for individual psychotherapy also should apply to societies and how they can improve. We have multiple mechanisms already in place to try to improve society, such as the creating policies in political parties, consulting universities and experts, and contributing to newspapers and others media that provide good outlets for analysis of our ills and the presentation of alternate solutions.

Nevertheless, our society needs to take a better look at itself from the perspective of facilitating positive change. Just as with individuals, each society is in transition and can be qualified for its developmental level, openness to positive change, good habits activated and bad habits inhibited, positive thinking and feelings, how it

copes with stress and tragedies, and how it deals with others.

I am proposing the societies can profit from analyses of their strengths and weaknesses in terms psychological processes that influence them and that can be improved by timely and effective strategies. Societies are governed by political processes, and they reflect social and economic forces, as well as adaptation to calamities related to the climate and geography. They consult specialists in all sorts of disciplines, but generally do not consider psychology as a key discipline that can help implement positive change. Positive psychology is beginning to have an impact this way, but not at the level of working with society itself as the unit that can be improved.

Typically, psychology has dealt with normal and abnormal behaviour experimentally but just abnormal behaviour clinically. **Positive psychology is a new psychological approach that studies and promotes optimal psychological well-being in all individuals.** Martin Seligman is its principal founder, and has developed a website that includes an educational component on positive psychology for by the public, for example, for use in schools. Recently, Seligman has written a book entitled "Flourish" that presents some conceptual innovations and clarifications, such as explaining the critical components in the field. These include positive relationships and emotions, finding meaning, accomplishing, and others. Moreover, he has developed a program called Flourish 2051 that is aimed at improving well-being through schools, business, and government.

Also, he has developed a program to help soldiers develop resilience. Ed Diener is among other key contributors to the approach of positive psychology, through his work on subjective well-being. He and colleagues have argued for national measures or accounts of well-being that could be tracked to inform policies. However, I am proposing a new way for positive psychology to help people.

Societies work in creating better laws and opportunities for the disadvantaged and disabled and to improve the physical and mental health of its members. However, do they consider frankly the best interests for its members at all levels? For example, for any one issue, are there self-serving interests in decisions arrived at, does one group (or groups) in society profit at the great expense of another, and so on? Sometimes the conservative tendencies in a society have the best solutions and sometimes the more liberal ones, but can they genuinely cooperate to find the best answers possible to problems that they face?

Positive psychology might be able to help this way because of its emphasis on developing optimally, promoting strength and resilience, and encouraging thriving. Perhaps working groups can be formed that lead to policy recommendations that are above the political fray and that aim toward the best for society in terms of psychological processes of its members and of the society as a whole.

You might consider me too idealistic, and believe that our society is not ready for this added layer either in monitoring the government or in its governance. However, think tanks, watchdogs, ombudsman, and review panels exist at multiple levels both in government and outside it. Why not consider one more group of this type that has the best interests of society at heart in an impartial way? Psychology has much to offer the individual, and also to government policies related to people needing its services. **Why can't psychology contribute to positive changes in society as whole, as well, for example, through what might be**

Original Published on October 26, 2011 on *Psychology Today*.
Link: http://www.psychologytoday.com/blog/rejoining-joy/201110/positive-society-psychology-i

POSITIVE SOCIETY PSYCHOLOGY II

Principles and Practices

In the prior blog entry, I have argued for the extension of positive psychology into the area of positive society psychology. In this second blog entry on the topic, I become more specific. (a) First, what are some practical ways that this new approach could be put into effect? (b) Second, what are some of the principles that positive psychology has to offer that can help society develop optimally, work toward a societal sense of subjective well-being, and maintain its gains through resilience?

Practices

At different levels, Western governments have independent financial watchdogs or auditors who point out yearly all the waste and poor decisions made by the government. In western countries, central banks, the Supreme Court, and other institutions have independent authority and do not have to answer to the government. Similarly, we can ask whether it is time to establish an independent nongovernmental organization think tank or even a government review board or panel that considers social, political, and economic policies from the psychological perspective. Perhaps it is time for societies to create the position of a society watchdog, an ombudsman heading some type of board or panel that functions for the good of society, being genuinely impar-

tial. This would be in terms of optimizing the psychological well-being related both to the members and groups of the society and to the psychological well-being of the society as a whole.

Moreover, if the government is involved in naming members to a board, government committees having equal members from the right and left should appoint them, so that if disagreements on nominees arise, compromises must be struck by the opposing sides in naming them. Whether governmental or non-governmental, the think tank, board, or panel would function from foundational principles related to positive psychology as applied to society as a whole and avoid the political scraps that often characterize and even paralyze society politics.

How would the positive society psychology group keep its relevance and not fall into doctrinaire habits? Most important, it would be open to positive change itself and not simply function in a vacuum according to unchangeable principles. In this regard, it would constantly seek to improve itself in terms of its underlying principles. Moreover, it would do the same in terms of how it undertakes its tasks and in terms of the recommendations that it makes. It would be fully open and accessible to the profession of psychology, related disciplines, the government, and especially the public. Therefore, it would create linkages with the public through town hall meetings and other venues, such as social media, which are not directly political.

An approach such as this would consider the needs of all members of the society, including those who suffer the most and need help due to either personal or contextual problems. At the same time, the positive psychology group would not be naïve and impractical. It would promote policies that would have safeguards to block individuals or groups from taking advantage or even working against and undermining the society and its fundamental values.

After gathering all the facts and data related to an issue that it is deliberating, the group would arrive at reasoned recommendations. The group would never arrive at decisions based on purely conservative or liberal ideologies in a reflexive manner without thinking. Rather, all conclusions made would consider all possible options from these perspectives and still reflect independence in thought and recommendations.

The positive psychology group would weigh the advantages and disadvantages of any recommendation made. It would act to assure that each recommendation considers all possible benefits compared to costs or losses. Also, the group would point out flaws and waste in existing government policies.

I would add that in all its endeavours it should take into account economic and social factors so that recommendations are practical even if idealistic. However, its deliberations and recommendations should not lead to policy directives in and of themselves. That would be for the government to decide. If the government

decisions about the group's recommendations do not please the public, people could react in the next round of voting.

Principles

The underlying principles to a psychology of positive society are difficult to elaborate because they need to be different from both positive psychology principles that have been developed for individuals and from general statements about the political and historical rights of individuals and peoples. That being said, the primary principles of positive society psychology should share these principles, which can be summarized, respectively, as the right to flourish and the right to have universal advanced forms of democracy.

The hardest part would be to find the optimal balance in individual and collective rights so that a balance is struck. **Ideally, the society promotes the optimal development of all its individuals and groups so that they work together toward societal flourishing and advanced and inclusive democratic functioning.** Another difficult part would be to avoid the extreme arguments that arise in the conservative-liberal divide and have both types help in the constant search for the optimal development of all individuals and of society as a whole.

Society forms an interconnected whole, and it needs to work to strengthen its evolutionary processes so that positive change takes place in natural and constructive ways. Ultimately, the goal of the working group on positive society psychology would be to suggest policies that, if implemented, would lead society to recommend without input from the group how to improve. Also for any society, there will be setbacks due to economic, social, climate, and geographical pressures and misfortunes. Therefore, another key goal of the group would be to help society develop coping and resilience mechanisms that keep it on track when stressors and calamities strike.

The idea being proposed merits further thought, and I look forward to your interactive suggestions. In the next blog entry in the series on positive society psychology, I project how this new scientific proposal might help both individuals and society in the year 2050.

Original Published on October 27, 2011 on *Psychology Today.*

Link: http://www.psychologytoday.com/blog/rejoining-joy/201110/positive-society-psychology-ii

POSITIVE SOCIETY PSYCHOLOGY III

Programs and Positives

The time is early in the year 2050. Belinda feels that she is in a straight-jacket both at home and at work. She works hard in both, and feels that she is getting no rest. Her husband has little interest in helping out at home, except to take the children to the playground where he would have fun with them. Her co-workers pile the work on her desk, knowing that they get along with the supervisor but she does not. In her mind, her universe is limited to stress and drudgery.

You must have experienced some of these feelings, because most people feel limited at times by their home life or work life. Granted, there are people who have it much worse than you or Belinda, for example, they are living in an abusive relationship, are unemployed, or both. However, the feelings of frustration, disappointment, and anxiety could be quite heightened for you even though others are in worse circumstances, and therefore you feel that there is no way out.

In a society informed by positive psychology, the following might transpire. Given your sense of being suffocated both at home and at work, you turn to the resources available to you on the internet. You recall the messages of positive psychology and refer to the approaches and techniques relevant to individuals that it had developed over the decades. Moreover, you dig into the topic of positive society psychology and learn how to deal with group issues such as you are having at home and at work. In both cases, psychology has emphasized the role of communication, for example, among the different parts of yourself, and how to communicate with others and resolve disputes. Also, you recall some of the lessons that you learned throughout your schooling in the decade beginning in 2020, that is, in your positive psychology programs on how to handle stress and to focus on solutions. Those programs had also taught you how to grow or flourish to an optimal level, whether in the role of a student, worker, partner, or parent.

Your Universe and Multiple Universes; Steps and Stages

You recall two principles that help explain how positive psychology works. (a) First, you remember that although you might feel stuck in yourself or in your world, you have to think outside of the framework of your world as it exists in the present. **There is not just your universe, but there are multiple worlds that could be constructed by yourself.** The one in which you are living in the present is one of them, but not the only one possible. You have the choice to analyze carefully your current world, see how to improve yourself, and see how to use the strategies that psychology teaches to help improve others. All this will help make your world better.

That being said, it is hard to predict where any changes to your world will bring you. In predicting the future, you might realize that there are several possible new worlds, or multiple universes. Because it is difficult to know in advance its exact nature, you have to be flexible and ready to accept different options. There is not one best path for you, and what might develop is relative. [Note to the reader, in this sense the term "relaverse" might be a better one than "multiple universes"]

(b) Second, your world might go through steps as it grows and these could be quite difficult to manage. Moreover, the steps might change quickly with little time for you to rest. However, in your positive psychology programs at school, you had learned that any type of growth might not be smooth. Systems might always be in change or resting before the next change. Ideally, systems are always on the edge of change and prepped to move in a positive direction. **Feeling stuck does not mean that positive change is impossible.** To the contrary, positive actions on your part can help your world grow in a positive direction.

In this sense, because in your world you seek constant positive change, your world might be in a constant state of instability or disequilibrium rather than stability and equilibrium. Living this way, there might be only isolated moments without change. You might have to get used to the idea of not trying to resist change. Moreover, resisting change could backfire and lead to negative change. [Note to the

reader: the concept of moments of change in a pattern of stability over time is referred to as "punctuated equilibrium." However, in terms of personal and societal growth, it is more likely that the optimal pattern reflects "punctuated disequilibrium."]

The time is late in the year 2050. You keep hope because you have learned attitudes and techniques that will help. Like Belinda, you start the path toward altering your world, changing yourself for the better and working to change others around. You had done this in the past and you will do it again in the future.

Improving Societies and Societal Relations

So far in this series of essays on positive society psychology, I have focused on the growth of individuals and of the society that we live in. However, just as couples can have disputes, so can societies. Indeed, our times are marked by brinkmanship, poor state relations, mini-wars, and great wars. The lingering effects of hatred drive people apart and facilitate further strife. In the future, an approach of positive society psychology might help societies to navigate the worst disputes and threats of war before conflagrations begin.

For example, I have implicated that the educational system would be influenced by the approach of positive society psychology. Everything possible should be done to encourage optimal psychological growth in children and parents in our society. Similarly, children in other societies should be exposed to a similar philosophy and its application. This will serve to help reduce the communication and cultural gaps across societies and help promote inter-cooperation instead of inter-competition.

Ideally, each society will be viewed as having the potential for constant positive change or transition and each one will have developed an approach and techniques to facilitate growth in other societies as well as its own, for example, by developing positive actions and policies and by learning how to control, alter, or inhibit the growth of negative ones.

Diplomats and representatives of all societies would be schooled in this mentality and would encourage the right way to alter any lapses in others. For example, any sign that children are being taught hate and destruction of another society would be stamped out in constructive ways by collective will and action before it can get too far.

This is my vision. This is your opportunity. In a certain sense, we can promote a better future and help overcome the troublesome signs in our present. Acting in the way indicated, or in a similar manner, would be positive for your psychology and for our society

Original Published on October 31, 2011 on *Psychology Today*.
Link: http://www.psychologytoday.com/blog/rejoining-joy/201110/positive-society-psychology-iii

Section X
Projects to Consider

I LOVE SCIENCE AND SCIENCE LOVES ME

Science is a Way of Thinking and Being

cience is a way of thinking and being. It is the application of our critical thought processes in effort to understand the world around us, using scientific methods. Science might be divided into disciplines such as physics, psychology, and biology, but it really is a unity. It is constantly being built by rigorous thought and research, so that it is a reflection of ourselves. By saying that not only do I love science but also that science loves me, I am indicating that the worlds we construct are part of ourselves and give back to us by their edification, inspiration, and community.

Scientists live science; they live critical and creative thinking, formulating practical and theoretical ideas, and testing them by gathering and studying data and evidence. Scientists love science; they are not emotionless automatons, but are passionate about their fields, share animatedly their ideas, have active personal lives, and seek harmonies within their interior universe and in the material universe.

Scientists know how important science is for the future of humanity and the planet. Their ultimate motivation is not only to achieve understanding for themselves and other scientists but also to help the public understand. They like seeing their ideas applied. Or, if they are doing basic, non-applied research, they know that even this type of research might help people one day or might contribute to the paths in knowledge creation that could help people one day.

Scientists love other disciplines. They respect greatly artists, historians, librarians, and health professionals, for example. Wherever there is rigorous, critical thought, great passion in work, and a helping attitude, scientists find common ground, not to mention that in their spare time they engage in activities such as singing, hiking and even climbing mountains, and writing poetry.

Science requires majestic effort and perseverance. Its discoveries are built on the collective work of other scientists and the gradual accrual of appreciating what works and what does not work as one proceeds. Scientists get lost behind the microscope, in data sheets, in the minds of patients, and the subject matter that they study. Their focus is intense and their reverie boundless. There is no joy equal to the "aha" experience of realizing something that has never been realized by anyone else before or in having a prediction confirmed in a scientific experiment. No wonder scientists like hiking and even mountain climbing! We love to spread the word to others, to present our ideas and data at conferences and to write up our literature reviews and studies for publication. This is like our music and our poetry.

Scientists talk in words and write in their native tongue or one in which they are familiar. However, they are really communicating in mathematics. Math could be a major part of their work, or perhaps the topic of focus. Moreover, they might not be conversant enough in math to find the equivalent mathematical expressions for their concepts, but because they are studying nature, this type of translation should be possible one day in all science. Scientists love mathematics and mathematics loves them.

I love psychology and psychology loves me. This is my scientific bag. Psychology is defined as the study of behaviour and its organization, but it is also about mind, brain-behaviour relations, and ways of living. Psychology aims to understand behaviour, and this also means when it gets disturbed and therapy can help. Therefore, there are two major branches of psychology— the research side and the practice side. Some of us are fortunate to be scientist-practitioners, like myself. It is hard work, being up to speed on the literature and contributing to it, and also meeting patients with a full presence and knowledge set in order to help them achieve their goals, and even help define those goals, as the need arises.

Children and teenagers need the best role models, including at home and at school. They look up to entertainers and athletes, as well as other people in the news, such as politicians, in particular. However, if they learned about how extraordinary is science and how dedicated and human are scientists, they might expand their search for role models. Astronauts make the perfect scientist role models, and there are famous scientists whom we all know, such as Einstein, but there are others whom children and scientists could appreciate, such those who contributed to the internet, the cell phone, and certain medicines. Indeed, children and teenagers are in contact with people who love science on a daily basis, such as their science teachers. We should develop sufficient resources for all children and teenagers to see the beauty and importance of science. There are so many initiatives this way, but do they reach all children and teenagers?

I am proposing to create a website called "I Love Science and Science Loves Me." Anyone who would like to contribute should let me know. It should include great descriptions of each of the scientific disciplines, testimonials by scientists, great videos of nature and scientists in action, and scenes of children and teenagers participating in science, such as school projects and science fairs. Given that I am a psychologist, it should include a psychological component. Of course, this could be one of the most interesting and visited areas of the website.

This project is a collective one. I have laid the seed, but it is all those people who are interested in it who will follow through. This is how people work and how science works. We share ideas and work and we build lasting edifices of community. Our bricks are ideas, and our mortar is talk. Our foundations are not in concrete and our structures are not in steel. Rather, our foundations are in the quality of our communications and our structures are in the shared pathways that we create, whether in science or any common task. We should live our lives in a way that brings us toward the loftiest levels both in ourselves and in others. **Nathan Hale said he regrets that he has one life to give for his country. Scientists think the same way. We regret that we have but one life to give for science.**

Original Published on May 31, 2011 on *Psychology Today.*
Link: http://www.psychologytoday.com/blog/rejoining-joy/201105/i-love-science-and-science-loves-me

SPORTINGTHON: GIVING HOPE

Helping people who are injured, ill, and with disability

Rehabilitation psychologists deal with psychological aspects of injury and illness. One of our defining features is that often we work in team with other professionals, including physicians. Also, we might work with the families involved. We attempt to understand the whole system.

It is so rewarding being a rehabilitation psychologist, but it is disheartening when I see a shortage in funding. Maybe this idea will help. Please let me know.

In watching students in one half of the gymnasium playing basketball with so much energy and other students playing indoor soccer, I wondered how we could harness that energy and spirit to help the needy who cannot get energy for much of anything. There are so many people with disabilities or in need of rehabilitation who require help. However, many of them do not have access to institutional or financial resources.

- A children's hospital with a large rehabilitation unit needs an advanced MRI machine for brain and body scans that would help injured and sick children, but funds are not available.
- John is in a serious motor vehicle collision and ends up paralyzed. He is ineligible for basic government services and his insurance services are limited.

- The local rehabilitation hospital is feeling the budget cuts and does not know how to cover the needs of its patients.
- Joanna develops a serious medical condition; not one government or insurance plan covers the cost of her medications. Her parents start to sell their house.
- A state brain association wants to have a well-known speaker come to its next meeting. He had been developing a program that could help the daily lives of people with brain injuries. But funds are lacking.

Perhaps there are ways to tap the energy of children and empower them to help those in need. For example, they could have schools organize basketball "Hoopathons" to raise funds. In addition, it would be helpful if people with disabilities could be involved in raising funds. They could be equally empowered by participating in sporting events for charitable purposes.

In the following, I describe some organizational principles of a proposed charitable organization that could be mounted to meet the challenge of:

a) raising funds for people with disabilities and in need of rehabilitation, and

b) empowering students and youths to participate in the fundraising, as well as people with disabilities.

1. The name of this nonprofit fund raising organization could be Sportingthon [e.g., sportingthon.org]. It would help organize events such as hoopathons, shootathons, and good old funathons involving sports. The pull heading could be "Helping Rehabilitation through Sporting Thons."

2. Although the major focus of the organization should be to help in the area of rehabilitation/disability, other tracks could be added as the organization evolves.

3. A possible mission statement might include: The primary organizational goal is to empower young people and/or people with disabilities (PWD)/enablements to take charge of raising funds for rehabilitation.

4. The children/PWDs undertaking the fundraising should have mentors helping them out, such as teachers or rehabilitation workers. Adults/helpers who would be helping organize should not do the work itself, unless there is no choice.

5. In addition, part of the empowerment process should include having the groups that raise funds help in deciding which organizations should get the funds that are raised (e.g., rehabilitation institutes, children's hospitals that include rehabilitation, head injury associations, trauma associations, pain associations).

6. Another possible component of the organization is that donors and other stakeholders work together to help raise funds. For example, insurers and banks could approach schools and organizations involving PWD.

7. The usual goal of sportathons is to raise funds at children's schools, and the amounts are limited. The goal of the present organization would be quite different. The students/PWD should not be responsible for getting sponsors themselves, and they should not be asked to raise money from their families.

8. Rather, sponsors/stakeholders would contribute monies to the organization, and once they are collected they would be released by the sporting events.

9. To further the empowerment process, the children/PWD should be informed of the financial amounts that their charitable activity has released, to where they have been disbursed, and how this has helped.

10. The funds could be earmarked for research, in particular. In this way, the organization would emphasize the importance of science to young people, too.

If Sportingthon can be launched, or if the idea for it otherwise inspires more fundraising activities in your community, we could see stories such as the following:

- To help a local wheelchair athlete go to a Special Olympathon, community fundraisers are organized.
- A city hospital no longer has to cut back staff that help people in the community re-integrate socially and vocationally after their stay in the trauma unit.
- A community organization of people with various disabilities is satisfied in its search for more funds to help make its point that they are people with enablements more than

disabilities and that they deserve a national program supporting their educational and retraining needs.

- Young people in one court no longer face jail time because rehabilitation and training services are available.
- A school board that prides itself on its charitable attitude to children helps students with disabilities.

If you would like to help discuss and launch the proposed charitable organization, or otherwise act to raise funds in your community for the cause described, contact me at asapil@glendon.yorku.ca, or 416-247-1625.

Original Published on February 17, 2011 on *Psychology Today.*
Link: http://www.psychologytoday.com/blog/rejoining-joy/201102/sportingthon-giving-hope

Generally, my blog entries examine self-help themes, and they could help people in rehabilitation and people with disabilities, as well. In addition, I have founded another nonprofit organization that you can check out as www.asapil.net.

WIKIWAYSOFLIVING

Gathering Knowledge for Ways of Living Life

Knowledge keeps growing and a major source of learning how to live comes from our searches on the web. However, there is too much for any one person to absorb, and the hits for any one question that we might ask in a search numbers in the millions. Moreover, the web does not include one site dedicated solely to improving our ways of living.

The danger is that when we seek advise on ways of living on the web, we find especially websites that are incomplete, not based on scholarship or science, or even try to take advantage of us commercially, politically, or other ways. For example, we might use alternative medicinal practices because apparent "classics" have been written about them and anecdotal evidence seems to support them. Alternatively, factors such as wanting to believe in them could help in their healing power so that they do seem to help even though by themselves they do not (the placebo effect). These types of decisions are not without dangers. For example, some people decided not to vaccinate their children against basic diseases because of an unfounded belief that the vaccines cause illnesses such as autism. Contemporary science has shown clearly the fraudulent and dangerous basis for this particular claim, but some people continue to risk the health of their children in a misplaced belief in the claim.

Instead of reverting to the past in face of the complexity of the present, we need to become better at knowledge-empowering ourselves—for example, in our studies, creativity, work, and personal life. Part of the internet world includes the phenomena of wiki sites. For example, there is one that is an encyclopedia, and its content quantity and quality are apparently outstripping classic encyclopedias. There are wikis for definitions. The word wiki has gained popular currency, and its use guarantees a certain allure, such as in the case of political leaks.

In this essay, **I am proposing that we develop a wiki for optimal ways of living in modern times, and I refer to it as "WikiWaysofLiving."** It should focus on the best ways of dealing with all aspects of our lives, from the personal to family to children, and from education to work to other social roles and activities. It should scour classics, such as the premodern traditions and texts, for advice on dealing with people, being moral, and living an adaptive and healthy lifestyle. However, it should search all eras for good advice, and especially strive to be inclusive of the new knowledge and wisdom that accumulates every day in contemporary times.

There is much to learn from contemporary study, science, technology, medicine, psychology, music, and other scholarly and creative disciplines that could help in our ways of living. There are wise traditions and premodern texts that deal with teaching us good ways of living, but also there are increasingly better ones every day from which we can learn. In addition, newer knowledge might even teach us how practices described in older traditions and texts are risky or negative for us and that these parts should be gently discarded from study and use.

If there was a wiki site doing this—collecting the core knowledge essential for optimal ways of living and continually updating it—it would be easier for people to consult it and live a better life. Moreover, a wiki such as this one might help avoid the fanaticism that accompanies certain negative beliefs in older traditions and texts, no matter where they have developed in the globe. If this wiki site is ever developed, psychology should be in the forefront. We are ways of living specialists, and we are part of a science that keeps improving insight for your best ways of living.

Original Published on April 26, 2012 on *Psychology Today.*
Link: http://www.psychologytoday.com/blog/rejoining-joy/201204/wikiwaysofliving

Section XI
Last Words For Your New Beginning

THE SMALLEST OF LIGHTS CAN
CAST THE LARGEST OF SHADOWS

Kindness is for all Seasons

How often have you heard the expression that she is a real light onto the world or he is such a bright light in the family? Being a light for other people does not mean that you are an outgoing, happy person but that you are a sensitive, caring person. You have a sensitive, caring side, but the stresses and the strains of the day could mask it. You might get up and look at your partner with an air of irritation thinking of the hard day ahead, or you might tell your children to hurry up and get ready for school without a pleasant wake-up greeting or hug. Or, you might not acknowledge correctly the act of a co-worker who saves you time and energy with her hard work and effort.

When you let your caring, sensitive, appreciative, and helpful side shine through, it might be expressed in the smallest of acts, such as offering a helpful hand to an older person in need, or a smile to a child who appears glum. When people react to your kindness, they light up, too, and your positive effects on people could become seared in your memories or theirs much more than any major accomplishment or success. **Kindness sets up a chain of reactions from one person to the other that might reach around the globe**, but a personal achievement stops at your desk, or perhaps your family's. Boasting about yourself cannot beat the feeling of having others complement you for your help and light.

You go through the day undertaking your daily responsibilities, and you might differ from the next person not in the acts undertaken in discharging them but in the attitudes that accompany them. One of you might remain pleasant no matter what the negative circumstances of the day and the other person might remain irritable no matter how positively the day is unfolding. To become the positive person of the two might take a small turn in attitude as the day begins that could lead to a major attitude shift as the day progresses. The little acts of understanding and kindness that you could give partner, child, or co-worker could ignite the light and lead to wanting to get on a daily basis the same positive reaction from people.

Being light in the sense of being kind and giving is its own reward. In addition, light grows and, when it starts shining, you cannot predict how strong it will get and which other person it will shine on. Being light is also the best reward that you can give to another person.

Also, giving light to others can last for generations. All your efforts and competitiveness might leave a permanent mark on society for some of you, but for most of you, but that is rare.

Moreover, even for those of you who have more of an effect, usually it is short term. Moreover, what people will remember most are the attitudes and acts of kindness, generosity, and respect that you carry with you and bring into the lives of others.

You might have the lowest paying job but spark a smile in others as you interact with them. Or, you might be the executive in chief but lower the light in other people by your lack of concern and empathy for them.

When it comes to acts of kindness and helping others, the smallest of lights can cast the largest of shadows. The fleeting smile to a stranger might unleash a fleet of good deeds in ways that you could not anticipate. Telling someone how a mistake can be a learning experience and then teaching them how not to make it again can lead to the best attitudes in the people around you. When life becomes a shared kindness and growing experience, it is easier to live and the benefits are incalculable. The smile that you give today might be the smile that reaches the highest heights or leads others to get there, and it could have repercussions that run around the world.

When you approach each moment of the day as the one where an act or attitude of kindness might have long lasting positive effects on yourself and on other people, your light will shine longer and stronger. People will notice and, moreover, the effects generated might last for generations through the chains of people affected over time. Life is ephemeral or transient for all of us, but it could be immemorial and immortal through your positive effects on the world via the kindness and caring that you shine on other people.

How can you improve kindness, caring, sensitivity, generosity, and related motivations? Part of the answer lies within yourself—you have triggers both to turn off the light and turn it on. By exploring what gets in the way of letting the internal light shine, the light might come on easier. Also, if you adopt the goal of being kinder and need help, there are ways of getting it, for example, by reading self-help books or blogs or by communication with family, friends, or mental health professionals.

You could be reading about kindness today because it is the holiday season that encourages it. However, for each and every day people need your acts of kindness. Whether they live around you or live around the world, they will receive benefits from the positive acts and kindness that you might give them. Perhaps begin with a smile and end with an avalanche.

Original Published on December 22, 2011 on *Psychology Today*.
Link: http://www.psychologytoday.com/blog/rejoining-joy/201112/the-smallest-lights-can-cast-the-largest-shadows

CHANGING STRESSES, BLOCKAGES, INSECURITIES, AND IMBALANCES

New You's Resolutions

The start of a new year can be a start of a new you, even if you begin small and slow. If you make realistic promises to yourself, they will be easier to realize. Moreover, you can always add others to fill them out along the way. You should treat each day as a new beginning, or start on that path.

To help you along, consider the following ways that positive changes can come about. First, I emphasize that much of the time stress can be dealt with positively. Stress is not only something out there because also it is something that we perceive according to our cognitive filters or schemes of the world and, of course, these can change for the better.

1. Changing Stress? Try seeing it differently

   a Stress enters your life
      i   But it is filtered through a schema, or structure of how you think
      ii That is, it is understood through the lens of your way of thinking
      iii For example, is the stress a challenge or is it overwhelming?

   b Person processes are involved
      i   The schema reflects past learning

      ii Also it reflects your personality, motivation, and mind

   c Response results
      i   Is it a passive reaction or an active or pro-active action?
      ii How does it take into account your context (relationships)?
      iii Are you acting responsibly, with a positive approach, or are there limits and barriers to address?

Second, if self-improvement is your goal, but you find it difficult, perhaps you can find ways of freeing the blocks in the way of your positive change. **The self is something that can keep growing; through reflection and effort, blockages can be removed**. The path to mental security is within your reach.

2. Changing Mental Blockage? Try the following

   a Mental Exploration
      i   Free the block
      ii Explore the reasons

   b Mental Building
      i   Find alternatives
      ii Put them together

   c Mental Security
      i   Try them out
      ii Keep close tabs on what works and what does not

Third, if mental insecurities are so deeply ingrained that much reflection and effort are required, there still are ways of achieving your New You's resolutions. If making simple mental jumps to the positive side is impossible, and even detours are hard to find there still could be ways to free the mental jams. This might need much mental exploration, insight, and effort, but your resolve is half the battle and psychology can help with the rest.

3. Changing Mental Insecurity? Use the following:

   a Mental Jumps
     i From the negative to a positive
     ii If there are no mental blockages, it's easy

   b Mental Jamborees
     i Might need a detour
     ii Jiggle around the problem
     iii You might need to explore if any blockage is serious

   c Mental Jam Busters
     i Might need a whole new way, path, habit, idea, or choice
     ii Because it's too clogged, leave your first path for a second
     iii But try to deal with the reasons behind the serious mental blockages or jam, too

Fourth, you might have too many or too difficult psychological defenses protecting past hurts or inabilities to deal with stress for your wishes and efforts to lead to positive changes. However, mental defenses are not permanent and you might be ready to deal with them. By letting out the hurt and insecurities in a controlled and helpful way, you can gain the beginning of understanding, new positives, and the new you that you are seeking. Mental balance means facing in an honest and open way what holds you back. When you start on that path, the new you will rejoice.

4. Changing Mental Imbalances? Try Pulling on the Positive

   a Mental Defense
     i Hold firm to negative
     ii Don't let go
     iii Use what you did in the past
     iv Get sick about it, regress

   b Mental Offense
     i Trick or attack the positive
     ii Deny, dissociate, delude
     iii Fantasize, rationalize, see it as a negative

   c Mental Balance
     i Pull back; reappraise
     ii Talk back; to the negative
     iii Pull hard; on the positive
     iv Praise yourself—for the good choice

Deciding to change for the better is the best choice, and taking steps toward this goal is a start to a New You. **Having positive resolutions to begin the year is a great idea, but there is no reason not to start now and keep at it every day.** After all, the New You will have it no other way.

Original Published on December 29, 2011 on *Psychology Today*.
Link: http://www.psychologytoday.com/blog/rejoining-joy/201112/changing-stresses-blockages-insecurities-and-imbalances

STEPPING UP AND ACTING ON

Taking Charge of Choice

Vinny was not sure about anything. Everything was a question mark for him. He struggled to make the most basic decisions. He did not see where his life was going. He had a humdrum job and also went from one date to another. He began to hit the bottle.

Andrea felt deceived by everything. She liked going to bars and meeting high rollers. She liked sexting with guys her friends considered losers. But after the exciting bed jousts she felt an internal emptiness. She did not know how to change her lifestyle. Increasingly, she turned to drugs.

You might be this person, stuck in a behavioral pattern either that you know needs change or that others keep telling you to change. In therapy, both Vinny and Andrea kept referring to their dysfunctional families. I emphasized to them that they had not reduplicated their family members' worst habits and that they had initiated therapy because of a deep desire to change. It took many sessions for them the chart their destructive behavior habits, their triggers, their underlying negative cognitions, beliefs, and self-blaming, and their failed efforts at resolving them. We explored their past histories and how they could take steps to change for the better.

"Stepping up" became one of the catchwords to characterize their change dynamic because it covered all the major areas of change that could take place. Stepping up is a phrase with multiple meanings and connotations, but all of them capture **the essence of changing for the better—taking the challenge [stepping up to the plate], moving up, for example, developmentally [taking a step up the stairs], and being active [stepping up the pace].**

To implement positive change, you need to be actively involved and even take the lead. Vinny and Andrea were stuck not because they did not have the ability to change but because they did not have the skill to get the process started.

The use of the stepping up metaphor in therapy changed that and it could help you, too. However, keep in mind that a metaphor can only serve as a short hand for a long journey in change and as motivating device to begin it and keep at it; the rest is up to you, and change takes your best effort, hard work, and vigilance.

This is where the second catchword that I used in therapy helped keep the change process on track and toward positive outcomes—that of "acting on." The phrase acting on evokes the notions of taking charge and acting for. Change does not happen because one passively wishes it but because one actively acts for it to happen, especially after different solutions or choices are formulated and the best one is chosen to try out.

Vinny and Andrea had developed the will to change but lapsed easily into old ways or bad habits. Vinny would drink on the week-ends in order to avoid hard decisions and adapting new ways. Andrea would take drugs to ease her way into the allure of cheap thrills. Both needed reminders of how to take their initial resolve and keep the change process fueled so that relapses were kept at bay.

We developed techniques to fit for their predicaments, based on behavioral techniques as natural relaxation strategies and cognitive and narrative techniques for understanding and dealing with their triggers. Then, we determined how best to have each of them to act on their plans and follow them to success.

Vinny and Andrea began to make progress in taking charge of their choices, of deciding for themselves instead of having bad habits that had emerged in their past decide for them. They used the metaphor of "acting on" to their advantage when self-doubt crept into their mentality.

However, for both of them, they felt that something was holding them back or getting in the way. It was as if the past held secrets that it did not want to reveal to them, and the secrets represented barriers that they had to overcome before being well on their way to more positive and more permanent change. At this point in therapy, a new catchword served as a powerful metaphor for changing for the better— that of "taking charge of choice." The metaphor evokes an active self that is acting to find the right path in behavior rather than a passive one waiting for bad habits to take over behavior.

Both Vinny and Andrea were encouraged to report to me their weekly efforts and setbacks and any revealing thoughts or feelings that they might have had. Andrea was the first to tell me about a fleeting thought that she had about her father telling her "It's only flesh" during times of his sexual abuse. We had explored abuse issues in therapy, but not her father's psychology in abusing her. These words became the secret terror that finally came out into her consciousness, and I helped her get through the worst of her regression due to the revelation. **Like Andrea, you can regain the strength of your positive journey in change and decide to never abdicate your role in deciding what was best for you and your future.**

Vinny also had a breakthrough in his control of bad habits and acting for himself rather than against himself and his best interest. He stopped using the bottle as an excuse for his bad habits once he recalled that as a child he had to protect his sister from his drunkard uncle who kept trying to abuse her. His parents did not believe them when they were told the first time it happened. In retrospect, he understood that the uncle brought gifts for the children and money for the family, being the proverbial rich uncle, and the parents acted to preserve this link.

The clients that I have described are composites, but the stories of change that they tell are valuable ones in which "stepping up," "acting on," and "taking charge of choice" serve as powerful metaphors toward promoting active change and in keeping it going in a positive direction. Life is not a metaphor nor is the therapeutic change process, but metaphors can help them along and cement their change for the better.

Original Published on January 13, 2012 on *Psychology Today*.
Link: http://www.psychologytoday.com/blog/rejoining-joy/201201/stepping-and-acting

LEAKS AND LANDMINES, LANDFILLS AND LANDSLIDES

From the Conscious into the Unconscious and Back

Your stream of consciousness is proceeding in its usual direction, giving you a rambling narrative of the day's events and ongoing tasks, perhaps with your concerns added about what is happening as the day unfolds.

However, you have a sudden change in your thoughts, behaviors, or mood and do not know why. Sometimes when you are alone thoughts unrelated to the day or present situation intrude and you are not sure why they seeped into your self-talk. Or, perhaps you are in a social interaction that seems to be going well, but you interject a thought or sentence that throws everyone off guard, including yourself. You wonder about the origins of these odd thoughts, feelings, and behaviors that could be quite troubling.

Because they might reveal hidden truths about you and your relationship with others, sometimes you build elaborate excuses for them because confronting and dealing with them would hurt too much. Or, you might just go on with the day and do not give them a second thought.

You might use a variety of other ways to defend against the psychological upset that they might generate, such as going in the opposite way that they had indicated. For example, perhaps you thought that you did not have much feelings about a colleague, but then at the work break you say something quite catty about her. In order

to make up for the gaff, the next day, you praise her way beyond what she deserves, and your colleagues seem confused.

Or, one of your parents or perhaps your partner asks you to help with a task and, instead of complying, you react quite angrily. In the end, you do much more than helping with the original request in order to make amends, and people are confused.

These examples illustrate the mind games that your unconscious and your conscious worlds play with you in the course of the day. Ideas, emotions, and intentions to act go back and forth between the conscious and unconscious as the day proceeds, and some are locked in the unconscious for quite long.

Defense mechanisms work like that—they help you to hide past hurts, cover up present hurts, or stop from happening hurts that might occur in the future. Defense mechanisms might even involve lies that you tell either to yourself or to others because they provide seeming short term psychological advantage, space, or gain.

We used to think that black holes in space were places where nothing could escape once anything was drawn into them. However, we have learned that matter/ energy can escape from them. The same applies to your unconscious. It is not a psychological place where everything that enters it remains forever inaccessible to you, or permanently unknown to you, forever buried, repressed, or otherwise forgotten. Rather, the unconscious is a place from which ideas, images, words, emotions, and intentions to act can emerge for your scrutiny.

Psychological movements in and out of consciousness could be either minor or major and also could be either controlled or uncontrolled. There are continual movements both ways—from the conscious to the unconscious and vice versa—as well as continual efforts to try to control them and their effects.

Leaks. When the emergence from consciousness is minor, it appears to be like a leak. The leak could occur in the day or it might be part of a dream. If you are ready to deal with the matter revealed in the leak—and the leak might have taken place for this very reason—your reaction to it will be controlled. You can learn from it and integrate its message into your positive growth instead of reacting with great worry and hurt.

Landmines. However, if the seepage from the unconscious to the conscious reveals serious underlying issues that have not been dealt with at all and you are not ready to confront and deal with them, great psychological turmoil might result. Therefore, I refer to this type of slippage into the conscious as a landmine instead of a leak. The deeper problems at the base of any landmine-type emergence from the unconscious might require much help (from family, friends, self-help books, etc.) and even psychotherapy.

What about psychological movements in the opposite direction, from consciousness into the unconscious? For example, according to Freudian theory, repression takes place in early life especially to remove from consciousness sexual desire for the opposite-sex parent. Many ideas, emotions, and intended actions are suppressed this way because of the hurt associated with them in one way or another.

Landfills. When the movement into the unconscious is a more controlled variety, it appears to be like a slow burial by landfill. The issue at hand is covered more slowly because it is less urgent. It might never re-emerge, especially if it is quite minor or becomes quite minor with time.

Landslides. However, when a psychological difficulty is so great that it needs immediate and massive removal from consciousness, the metaphor of a landfill does not work. Rather, you engage in a psychological movement from consciousness to the unconscious that resembles a landslide rather than a landfill. The matter that required such urgent and extreme psychological burial or rerouting might continue to haunt you without you ever knowing directly what it is or knowing how to deal with it.

Seeking help from and communication with family, friends, therapists, and readings such as in these blogs, along with your desire to grow and change for the better, can help with problems in the psychological movements from the conscious to the unconscious and vice versa. By working with them, in the sense of letting them inform you and important others in your life about your problems, you can take beginning steps in the creation of more solid foundations in your psyche.

Original Published on January 26, 2012 on *Psychology Today.*
Link: http://www.psychologytoday.com/blog/rejoining-joy/201201/leaks-and-landmines-landfills-and-landslides

THE DIABOLICAL AND THE DIALOGICAL

Fighting Evil on the Inside and on the Outside

The elephant in the room is the evil in the world that is all around you. You try to live through the stresses of the day, and have little room to deal with the stresses of your family, let alone those of the community, country, and world.

So the evil in the world that you read about or hear about becomes part of the background noise in your life as you deal with matters more urgent for you. You might be too busy dealing with project deadlines, getting the children off to school, and helping friends with their social lives to worry about the hate and evil that is everywhere.

A lot of evil resides in the people, politics, and clash of cultures around you, and it seems insurmountable. For example, how much can you do to help, as one person, in face of the evil intentions of whole countries? Alternately, the neighborhood might be ruled by gang warfare, and your children live in fear and you feel helpless. Or, some politicians in government might be corrupt and steal money from accounts destined for people in need, leaving you in worse shape than ever.

There is another type of evil that you might encounter—the potential for *you* to be evil; the potential to express the worst bad habits that greatly hurt other people reside in all of us. You might say to yourself that this is impossible, but who knows what circumstances the future might bring to you and who

knows how your psychological integrity might change because of them.

Or, at the other extreme, already you could be acting in the worst way, such as in abusing a child or a partner, and you know it as the wrong thing to do as much as other people. But you do not care to stop nor do you care about the consequences that result for the people who you hurt.

Or, you might perceive in a cold, calculating way that evil is necessary in a particular situation and expressing it might even bring you a certain pleasure (think sadism). [This type of evil is not the subject of this blog; but people who have this type of problem need much help to change their behavior.]

Sometimes you might perceive aggressive or evil intentions in other people when in fact the intentions are not this bad. Think of when you have attributed the worst intentions to people and ended up being wrong.

The same thing can happen about peoples or countries perceptions of other peoples or countries. Unfortunately, you or even a country or people could end up acting out of anger, hate, or evil for quite inappropriate and incorrect reasons.

You might think that I am exaggerating your potential for evil. To the contrary, because evil is a reality and can even reside in each of us, it is best to confront that reality and have each of us become aware of the potential for evil to manifest and learn how to deal with it.

Anger can disintegrate into evil without much effort, especially when you are in the middle of expressing anger. **Anger is an emotion that indicated frustration, but it does not come with a plan to solve the frustration.** That has to come from you and you might not have the will, resources, or ways of doing this effectively without help.

Anger management is a common psychotherapeutic topic; and many of the techniques related to anger management can be used to manage its most extreme version—the impulse to evil. **Good anger management skills begin with good communicating with others and good communication with the self.**

Good communication with others might help you get through tough times and offer you options that you had not been aware of. Good self-talk could spark you to find better paths than retreating into anger, hate, or evil.

Anger and evil reactions can be controlled by positively building yourself and your situation, and you can learn to do this better. Moreover, you can get other people to help you with it. Sometimes something as simple as a caring response by other people can help defuse your anger and turn things around.

For example, instead of perceiving your situation as a dead-end for which you have to strike out at others to get some semblance of a solution, you could learn of a different way and resist striking out and causing harm to others. The more you learn anger control, coping mechanisms, and how to solve problems, the more you leave the path that leads to anger as a first response.

As you build your psychological positives, there is less room for negatives. As you grow stronger psychologically and in the direction of using good habits, the temptation to use bad habits lessens. Anger becomes less of an option, as does evil. By your positive growth, you greatly reduce a place for the potential for evil that you harbor to find an active place in your psychology.

As you become more equilibrated and pleasant, you encourage the same in others. Your growth feeds their growth; other people become better at developing positive habits, anger management skills, evil control, and resistance of falling into bad habits.

The approach that I am advocating is that the war against evil begins at home—this approach gives less chance for evil to manifest and more chance that it will be successfully altered or resisted in other people who want to act in evil ways.

Of course, there are times when peoples and countries need to combat great evil directly. However, peoples or countries that live a philosophy of anger control amongst themselves can better coordinate in acting together toward combatting external evils. Once more, evil control starts at home.

Original Published on February 2, 2012 on *Psychology Today*.
Link: http://www.psychologytoday.com/blog/rejoining-joy/201202/the-diabolical-and-the-dialogical